SpringerBriefs in Health Care Management and Economics

Series editor
Joseph K. Tan, McMaster University, Burlington, ON, Canada

More information about this series at http://www.springer.com/series/10293

Yaeko Mitsumori

The Indian Pharmaceutical Industry

Impact of Changes in the IPR Regime

Springer

Yaeko Mitsumori
Osaka University
Osaka, Japan

ISSN 2193-1704 ISSN 2193-1712 (electronic)
SpringerBriefs in Health Care Management and Economics
ISBN 978-981-10-6789-1 ISBN 978-981-10-6790-7 (eBook)
https://doi.org/10.1007/978-981-10-6790-7

Library of Congress Control Number: 2017956762

Printed on acid-free paper

This Springer imprint is published by the registered company Springer Nature Singapore Pte Ltd.
The registered company address is: 152 Beach Road, #21-01/04 Gateway East, Singapore 189721, Singapore

Contents

Chapter 1
Introduction

This chapter explains why the author selected India as her research subject and goes on to discuss the roles of the World Trade Organization (WTO) and the Agreement on Trade-Related Aspects of Intellectual Property Rights (TRIPS). This chapter also outlines the research subject and objectives.

1.1 Background

The Agreement on Trade-Related Aspects of Intellectual Property Rights (TRIPS), which came into force in 1995, is an international agreement administered by the World Trade Organization (WTO) (Note 1: TRIPS). The Agreement sets out the minimum standards of protection to be provided by each member (Note 2: Minimum Standards). Each member country, whether it is a developed or a developing country, is required to apply the provisions of the Agreement to its own intellectual property-related legislation.

In the formulation stages, developed countries, especially the US, argued forcefully for strong intellectual property (IP) protection. As a result, the Agreement required every member country, including developing countries, to introduce the kind of IP protection frameworks that advanced countries were adopting at that time, including product patents #1. Some countries, notably developing countries, argued that the IP frameworks required under TRIPS posed a high hurdle for less advanced economies.

For advanced countries, IP protection plays a vital role in fostering their industries. IP functions as a driving force for economic development. For the pharmaceutical industry, which demands very high levels of technology, patents—particularly product patents—are extremely important because they protect ownership and marketing rights to new chemical entities (NCEs) and biologics over many years (Note 3: Importance of Patents for the Pharmaceutical Industry).

Y. Mitsumori, *The Indian Pharmaceutical Industry*,
SpringerBriefs in Health Care Management and Economics,
https://doi.org/10.1007/978-981-10-6790-7_1

Some earlier studies showed that introduction of product patents in developing countries tended to hamper industrial development. In 1996, La Croix and Kawaura examined prices of pharmaceutical company stocks before and after introduction of product patents in Japan and Korea, and they found that introduction of product patents in developing countries was likely to have a negative impact on industrial development.

TRIPS came into effect in 1995. The Agreement required not only developed countries but also developing ones to introduce intellectual property protection frameworks. However, developing countries were given an extended transition period of 5–10 years over which to introduce such frameworks.

Even after TRIPS took effect, not only developing countries but also several other stakeholders, including international NGOs/NPOs, developed countries, academics, and patient communities expressed concerns about the potential negative impact that the TRIPS standards could have on the pharmaceutical industries in developing countries.

India, which is home to the world's second largest population, is still categorized as a developing country. As a former colony of Great Britain, it has a long history of intellectual property protection based on the British system. The history of patent law in India is said to date from 1911, when the Indian Patents and Designs Act, 1911 was enacted [1].

However, the 1911 law was amended in 1970 as part of a sequence of domestic industrial protection policy measures. Its replacement, the Patents Act, 1970, came into force on April 20, 1972. One notable feature of the new law was that it allowed only "process" patents with regard to inventions relating to drugs, medicines, food, and chemicals (Note 4: The Patents Act, 1970).

Under the Patents Act, 1970, Indian pharmaceutical companies were permitted to "legally" manufacture pharmaceutical products which had patent protection in other countries. As a result, the Indian pharmaceutical industry developed so rapidly that, by 2005, it had become the fourth largest (by volume) pharmaceutical industry in the world.

India is a foundation member of the WTO. In 2005, as required by the provisions of the TRIPS Agreement, it revised its patents legislation and reintroduced product patents [2].

Once the country decided to reintroduce a product patents regime into the Indian Patents Act, many stakeholders expressed concerns about the potential negative impact of introducing product patents into the Indian pharmaceutical industry. For example, drug prices could soar; Indian pharmaceutical companies would no longer be permitted to produce currently patented pharmaceutical products.

This study started with selecting "India"—which has a very interesting background in terms of both its pharmaceutical industry and intellectual property protection schemes—as a case for analyzing the impact of introducing product patents on industries.

1.2 Trend of Indian Pharmaceutical Industry and Indian Patent Policies

1.2.1 Trend of Indian Pharmaceutical Industry

In the wake of TRIPS enforcement, Indian pharmaceutical companies were obliged to depart from their conventional business model—exclusively producing generic drugs #2 utilizing reverse engineering #3 technology.

Annual reports of leading Indian pharmaceutical companies show that, from the mid-1990s, these companies began increasing R&D investment and started to develop value-added generic drugs and/or new chemical entities (NCEs). They were apparently seeking to avoid the negative impacts of patent introduction on business performance by developing branded generic drugs #4 and brand-name drugs #5, in addition to the conventional simple generic drugs.

1.2.2 TRIPS Enforcement and Background to Introduction of Product Patents

India has had some kind of intellectual property protection system since colonial times. Immediately after the country won its independence from Britain in 1947, the domestic pharmaceutical industry was immature. Then, foreign pharmaceutical companies began entering the Indian market and would soon dominate it.

According to "The Current Status of the Indian Pharmaceutical Industry," compiled by the International Committee of the Japan Pharmaceutical Manufacturers Association (JPMA), foreign-owned companies commanded 68% of the Indian pharmaceutical market as of 1970 [3].

According to "Pharmaceutical Industry and the Indian Patent Act with Particular Reference to Madras High Court's Novartis Rulings," in 1960, drug prices in India were the highest in the world [4].

Then Prime Minister Indira Gandhi, disappointed at seeing the Indian pharmaceutical market dominated by foreign-owned companies, implemented a series of policy measures aimed at forcing those companies out (Note 5: Protectionist Policies Introduced by the Government of Indira Gandhi).

An important aspect of the policy package was passage of the Patents Act, 1970 (effective April 1972) (Note 6: The Patents Act, 1970).

India's Patents Act, 1970 exempted "pharmaceutical, food and agricultural chemical products" from product patent compliance, and only "process" patents in these fields were protected under the law [5].

The exemptions prompted a steady exodus by foreign pharmaceutical companies out of the Indian market [6].

With product patent protection exempted under the Patents Act, 1970, Indian Pharmaceutical companies in India could "legally" manufacture brand-name drugs which were protected in other countries and market them both domestically and in overseas markets without infringing patents [7].

Since the Patents Act, 1970 allowed many new, local companies to enter the Indian pharmaceutical industry, fierce competition erupted in the domestic market, pushing drug prices ever lower. In due course, India would boast some of the lowest prices in the world [6].

Due to their affordability, drugs manufactured by Indian companies gained strong acceptance both at home and abroad. That is why the Indian pharmaceutical industry developed so rapidly and successfully.

However, as mentioned above, India, as a foundation member of the WTO, was eventually obliged to revise its existing patent law into a TRIPS-compatible, international patents system by 2005.

Despite many expressions of concern, the Indian government moved—by way of an external pro forma measure—to introduce product patents by January 1, 2005, the deadline set by TRIPS. In order to protect the Indian pharmaceutical industry against penetration of the domestic market by foreign-owned companies, the Indian government inserted a safeguard article, Section 3 (d), into the Patents (Amendment) Act, 2005. Section 3 (d) strictly limits the scope of patentability [8].

1.2.3 Discussion around Introduction of Product Patents into the Indian Patent Regime

As mentioned, after TRIPS required every country, including developing countries, to introduce product patents, various stakeholders voiced concerns [9].

There were three main areas of concern:

1. High drug prices and access to drugs: If product patents were introduced in developing countries, drug prices would increase; as a result, lower-income people in those countries would lose access to drugs.
2. Constraints on industrial development: If product patents were introduced in developing countries, local industrial development would suffer.
3. Penetration by foreign-owned companies: If product patents were introduced in developing countries, foreign-owned companies would penetrate into domestic markets, which would be swamped with overseas-manufactured products.

Because Indian pharmaceutical companies, taking advantage of advanced technology and low production costs, were exporting large volumes of inexpensive but high-quality drugs to Third World countries, international NGOs/NPOs, including Médecins Sans Frontières (MSF) #6, raised objections to introduction of product patents in India. According to MSF, Indian pharmaceutical products accounted for some 80% of the drugs sent by MSF to African countries to support the health of impoverished local communities [10].

Meanwhile, the Indian Drug Manufacturers' Association (IDMA) (Note 7: IDMA), an industry association of small to medium-sized pharmaceutical companies, also objected to introduction of product patents in India, arguing that the Indian pharmaceutical industry would be harmed by such introduction [11].

Their discussion points included the following:

1. Drug prices in India would increase.
2. Foreign-owned companies would penetrate into the Indian market.
3. If product patents were to be introduced in India, Indian pharmaceutical companies would no longer be able to reverse engineer patented drugs #7 and manufacture so-called generic drugs (actually, copycat drugs).
4. Since there were no product patents in India, local pharmaceutical companies reverse engineered patented drugs and started developing generic drugs earlier than any other country's pharmaceutical manufacturers. However, if product patents were to be introduced in India, those companies, like their foreign counterparts, would be forced to wait until the patents of targeted brand-name drugs expired. In such a regulated market, Indian pharmaceutical companies would cease to be competitive.

As mentioned above, the opponents unanimously argued that the Indian pharmaceutical industry would lose its edge. Foreign-owned companies countered that argument by suggesting that, if product patents were introduced in India, local pharmaceutical production would not decline but, rather, would be energized and accelerated.

Taking into account the concerns expressed by various stakeholders, including industry associations and international NGOs/NPOs, the Indian government inserted Section 3 (d) into the Patents (Amendment) Act, 2005. Section 3 (d) rejects patent applications submitted by foreign-owned companies by restricting the scope of patentability [12].

The Indian government intentionally inserted Section 3 (d) in order to protect Indian pharmaceutical companies against penetration of the Indian market by foreign-owned companies.

1.3 Research Subject and Objectives of This Study

Some prior studies suggest that introduction of stringent patent systems, including product patent regimes, in developing countries tends to inflict deleterious impacts on local pharmaceutical industries and cause their decline.

In contrast, data from financial reports and annual reports of leading Indian pharmaceutical companies show that those companies continued to achieve healthy development, even after 2005, the year in which product patents were introduced in India.

If the Indian pharmaceutical industry continues to develop, avoiding the negative impacts from introduction of product patents indicated by some prior studies, analysis of the causes/factors in their healthy development could provide guidelines for strategies/tactics to help other developing countries find a way to balance international cooperation against domestic industry development.

One possible approach might be found in Section 3 (d), which the Indian government inserted into the Patents (Amendment) Act, 2005. Did Section 3 (d) play an important part in enabling India to maintain a responsible stance in the international community while also protecting Indian pharmaceutical manufacturers against incursions by foreign-owned companies and allowing the local pharmaceutical industry to continue to flourish? Another possible factor in the ongoing success of the Indian pharmaceutical industry could be the changing of companies' business models: leading pharmaceutical manufacturers adapted their models to suit the new business environment that was brought about by introduction of product patents in the Patents (Amendment) Act, 2005.

Financial reports and annual reports show that leading Indian pharmaceutical companies, around the mid-1990s, began increasing R&D investment and initiating new drug development. Did the introduction of product patents in 2005 trigger a change in the business models of these major players? This study is aimed at exploring those two research questions.

In the wake of TRIPS enforcement, other *newly industrialized countries (NICs)* and developing countries started introducing product patents into their own patent regimes. This study may provide some guidance to help those countries to formulate patent regimes appropriate to their current status. In that sense, this study may have significant value.

References

1. Indian Patent Office Website, "Brief about Indian Patent System," http://www.ipindia.nic.in/history-of-indian-patent-system.htm (accessed 2017).
2. WTO Website, "Frequently asked Questions about TRIPS in the WTO," https://www.wto.org/english/tratop_e/trips_e/tripfq_e.htm.
3. "The Current Status of the Indian Pharmaceutical Industry" (research materials, no. 400, The Japan Pharmaceutical Manufacturers Association [JPMA], July 2009): 15.
4. Mika Yamana, "Pharmaceutical Industry and the Indian Patent Act with Particular Reference to Madras High Court's Novartis Rulings," *Patent Studies*, no. 44 (Sept. 2007): 41.
5. Shiro Mori, "The Current Status of IP Protection in India: In the Wake of Revision of Patent Law in 2005, Indian Pharmaceutical Companies One After Another Set Up R&D Centers," *Nikkei BP IP Awareness* (Dec. 2007).
6. Kazuki Minato, "Indian Pharmaceutical Industry – Structural Background for Development and Changes after TRIPS," *Japanese Generic Medicine Market and Indian & Chinese Pharmaceutical Industries*, ed. Kensuke Kubo (Institute of Developing Economies-JETRO, 2007), 34.
7. Kazuhiro Kawabata, "Overseas Penetration by Indian Pharmaceutical Companies," Chap. 15 in *The Current Status of Indian Pharmaceutical Industry* (Yakuji Nippo, Yakuji Nippo Limited, Sept. 11, 2007).
8. Keiji Iwata, "The Effect of the Indian Patent Law Amendment," *Patent* 61, no. 2 (Feb. 2008): 43–44.

9. "TRIPS, Patents and Access to Medicines: Proposals for Clarification and Reform" (briefing paper, Third World Network, June 2001).
10. Médecins Sans Frontières Website, http://www.doctorswithoutborders.org.
11. Indian Drug Manufacturers' Association (IDMA) Website, https://idma-assn.org/about-idma.html.
12. Hiroko Yamane, *Interpreting TRIPS: Globalisation of Intellectual Property Rights and Access to Medicines*. (Iwanami Shoten, 2008), 350.

Chapter 2
Historical Background and Current Status of Indian Pharmaceutical Industry and Indian Patents Regime

This chapter discusses the historical background and the current status of the Indian pharmaceutical industry and India's patents regime. First, this chapter presents an analysis of the current global standing of the Indian pharmaceutical industry. Then, it describes some notable features of intellectual property in relation to the pharmaceutical industry, as compared to the Information Technology (IT) industry. Next, it looks at the Indian pharmaceutical industry from the aspects of market share, disease profiles, regulations, and sales profiles. It concludes with a description of the historical background to the Indian regime, including the Indian Patents Act, 1970 and the Indian Patents (Amendment) Act, 2005.

2.1 Status of the Indian Pharmaceutical Industry

In response to the adverse impact of the 1991 Balance of Payments crisis on economic performance, the Indian government implemented a series of economic reforms. Due to the success of those policy measures, the economy experienced GDP growth of 6.8% (on average) between 1991 and 2008 [1].

The country achieved high economic growth between 2005 and 2007: 9.5% in FY2005, 9.6% in FY2006, and 9.3% in FY2007. However, India's growth rate slowed to 6.7% for 2008 as a result of the global recession triggered by the Lehman Brothers collapse. In the wake of the "Lehman Shock," a number of emerging economies suffered from negative growth, but India managed to maintain a positive trend, recording 8.4% growth rates for both FY2009 and FY2010, 6.7% in FY2011, and 5.6% in FY2012 (Table 2.1).

In recent years, India has enjoyed the world's highest rate of economic growth. According to the World Bank's "Global Economic Prospects, June 2016: Divergences and Risks," released in June 2016, India recorded 7.2% growth in 2014

Y. Mitsumori, *The Indian Pharmaceutical Industry*,
SpringerBriefs in Health Care Management and Economics,
https://doi.org/10.1007/978-981-10-6790-7_2

Table 2.1 India basic economic indicators by JETRO

Items	2012	2013	2014
Real GDP growth rate	5.6%	6.6%	7.2%
Nominal GDP	99,513 (bil Rs)	112,728 (bil Rs)	124,882 (bil Rs)
Per capita nominal GDP	1,483 (US$)	1,491 (US$)	1,612 (US$)
Industrial production index	1.1 (%)	$^{\Delta}$0.1 (%)	2.8 (%)
Consumer price index	10.3 (%)	10.0 (%)	5.9 (%)
Unemployment ratio	3.6 (%)	3.6 (%)	3.6 (%)
Exports	300,150 (US$mil)	314,416 (US$mil)	309,932 (US$mil)
Imports	490,204 (US$mil)	448,832 (US$mil)	447,087 (US$mil)

Source: India Basic Economic Indicators, JETRO

and 7.6% in 2015. The World Bank estimated that the country would achieve 7.6% growth in 2016 and 7.7% in 2017 and 2018 [2].

According to "Indian Pharmaceutical Industry: An Overview," the contribution of the pharmaceutical sector to India's GDP is 2% [3].

Kadokura, in his article "Indian Pharmaceutical Industry Standing on a Turning Point," noted that the pharmaceutical industry and the IT industry are major drivers of India's economy, jointly providing 2.9 million new jobs per year [4].

Takeda, in his report, mentioned that Indian's two major industries after IT are "medical care" and "medicines" [5].

According to "OECD Health Policy Studies: Pharmaceutical Pricing Policies in a Global Market," the total global pharmaceutical market in 2006 was worth US$608 billion, with the US market holding a 45.1% share [6].

Table 2.2 and Fig. 2.1 show the world pharmaceutical market by country, as of 2007, with the US commanding about 38% and Japan, the US, and Europe jointly accounting for some 80% of the total market. Although India is shown as accounting for only 1%, its pharmaceutical market has been expanding rapidly.

According to IBEF, the Indian pharmaceutical industry as of 2016 was worth US$36.7 billion, and it is expected to expand at an annual growth rate of 13% between 2015 and 2020, when it is projected to reach US$55 billion [7].

As of 2016, the Indian pharmaceutical sector accounted for 2.4% of the global pharmaceutical industry in value terms and 10% in volume terms [8].

There are several reasons for the rapid expansion of India's pharmaceutical industry, some of which were highlighted in an article by Toshimitsu Kurogi, former representative director of Torrent Pharma Japan [9].

Strengths of India and its people, according to Kurogi:

1. The Indian pharmaceutical industry has been rapidly expanding in line with the rate of growth of India's economy. There is still a lot of potential for further growth in India.
2. India has a plentiful supply of trained high-technology human resources. Labor costs are low (research, development, and production).
3. India's politics are quite stable.
4. India is a contract-based society, making it easy (or, at least, easier) to conduct business there.

Table 2.2 Top 14 countries based on pharmaceutical market share

	Market share (%)
US	37.6
Japan	10
France	5.5
Germany	5.3
Italy	3.4
China	3.2
UK	2.9
Spain	2.7
Brazil	2.5
Canada	2.4
Mexico	1.4
Turkey	1.4
South Korea	1.3
India	1.2
Rest of the world	19.2
Total	100

Source: Visiongain, "Indian Pharmaceutical Market Outlook 2009–2024" (2009): 32

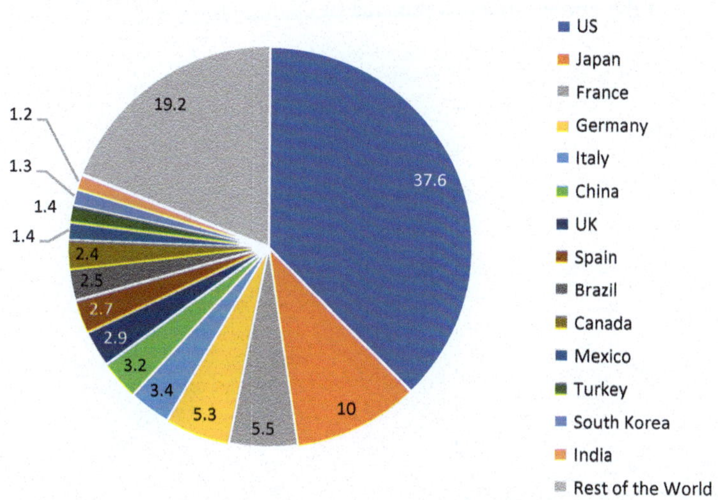

Fig. 2.1 Top 14 countries with large pharma markets (*Source*: Visiongain, "Indian Pharmaceutical Market Outlook 2009–2024" (2009): 32)

5. English is a semi-national language.
6. There are more than several hundred million individuals with higher education qualifications.
7. Indians are generally good at mathematics and academic levels in science and technology are generally high.

William Greene of the US International Trade Commission also pointed out some strengths of India and its people:

Strengths of India's pharmaceutical industry:

- Cost advantages
- Large pool of highly trained personnel
- The largest number of US FDA-approved facilities (75)
- TRIPS compliance (patents regime)
- Lower operating margins
- Drug costs a fraction of those in Western countries
- Growing biotechnology industry
- Reverse engineering skills
- Largest number of DMFs
- Biodiversity
- Strong IT skills for research data management
- Political stability
- Strong marketing and distribution networks
- Well-established network of laboratories [10]

Figure 2.2 shows a conceptual diagram of the global pharmaceutical industry. The vertical axis shows technology levels, the horizontal axis shows drug prices, and the size of the circle indicates the size of each country's market.

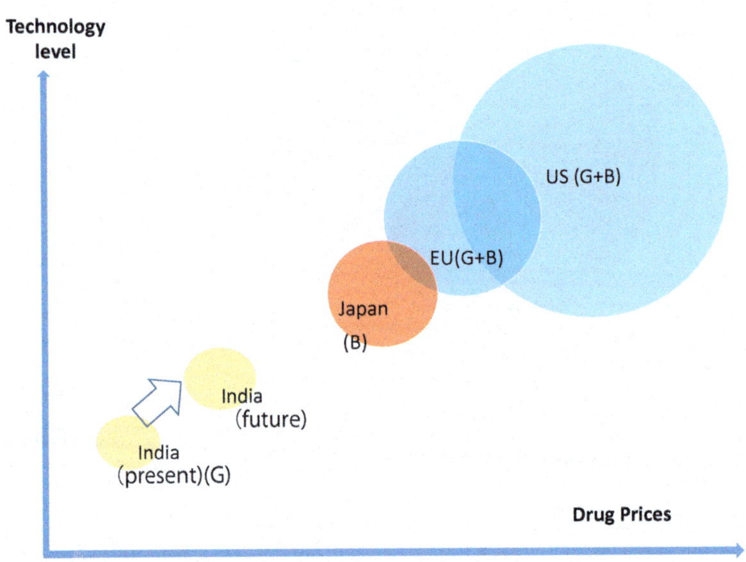

Fig. 2.2 A correlation diagram among technology levels, drug prices, and market sizes of world pharmaceutical markets (conceptual diagram) (*Source*: The author created this chart based on "Future Vision of the Pharmaceutical Industry" and other materials)

According to "IMS World Review Executive," North America commands almost half (44.3%) of the world pharmaceutical market, followed by Europe (28.8%) and Japan (9.9%). When the component countries of Europe are treated as individual countries, Japan becomes the world's second largest market after the US.

According to "Future Vision of the Pharmaceutical Industry: The Mission and Issues toward 2015," the average drug price in the US is the highest in the world, partly because the US market is a free market. If the US average drug price is set at 1.0, that of Germany is 0.52, France 0.49, UK 0.47, and Japan 0.33 [11].

In Fig. 2.2, "G" stands for generic drugs (off-patent drugs) and "B" stands for brand-name drugs (patented drugs). Pharmaceutical products are basically divided into those two groups.

In a general sense, the US and Europe are mixed markets, with both brand-name and generic drugs. Whereas the Japanese market was formerly dominated by brand-name drugs, in recent times the proportion of generic drugs has been growing rapidly, partly as a result of Japanese government policy measures aimed at expanding the use of generics. According to a press release issued on September 29, 2016, by the Japan Generic Medicines Association, the proportion of generic drugs in Japan had reached 60.1% on a volume basis and 38.4% on a value basis [12].

In contrast, the Indian market is predominantly one of generic drugs. According to IBEF, generics account for 70% of the Indian market, with brand-name drugs making up only 9% [13].

There are several yardsticks for measuring technology levels. One is new drug development capability. "Current Status of and Issues Surrounding the Pharmaceutical Industry—In Order to Provide Better Medicines" listed the origins of the world's 100 best-selling drugs between 2003 and 2013 (Table 2.3).

Table 2.3 Top 10 origin countries by inventors

1	US
2	UK
3	Japan
4	Switzerland
5	Germany
6	Belgium
7	France
8	Denmark
9	Sweden
10	Israel

Source: Office of Pharmaceutical Industry Research (OPIR), "Current Status of and Issues Surrounding the Pharmaceutical Industry: In Order to Provide Better Medicines" (Japan Pharmaceutical Manufacturers Association [JPMA], 2015): 16

Table 2.4 Top 10 origin countries by patentees

1	US
2	Switzerland
3	Japan
4	UK
5	Germany
6	Denmark
7	Belgium
8	France
9	Sweden
10	Israel

Source: Office of Pharmaceutical Industry Research (OPIR), "Current Status of and Issues surrounding the Pharmaceutical Industry: In Order to Provide Better Medicines" (Japan Pharmaceutical Manufacturers Association [JPMA], 2015): 16

By country of inventors, Japan comes in third behind the US and the UK [14].

By country of patentees, Japan stands in third place behind the US and Switzerland [14] (Table 2.4).

The "Current Status of and Issues Surrounding the Pharmaceutical Industry: In Order to Provide Better Medicines" report also listed the number of molecules in the drug development pipelines #8 by country between 1999 and 2013. According to the report, Japan had the second largest number after the US.

The other countries on the list were the UK, Switzerland, Germany, France, Canada, Korea, Denmark, Israel, and India.

The report noted that, recently, Korea, India, and Israel have been gearing up R&D activities, and the numbers of molecules in their respective pipelines have been increasing rapidly [15].

"Future Vision of the Pharmaceutical Industry: The Mission and Issues toward 2015" compared R&D investment amounts between 1996 and 2005 among US companies, European companies, and Japanese companies. According to the report, the average US company invested US$32 billion during the decade, and the average investment for European companies was US$34 billion. In stark contrast, the average investment for Japanese companies was only US$8.5 billion during that period. The report pointed out that in order to improve their competitiveness, Japanese pharmaceutical companies should expand R&D investment by strengthening their income generation frameworks [16].

"Future Vision of the Pharmaceutical Industry: The Mission and Issues toward 2015" also listed by country the number of papers published in highly influential journals with high impact factors #9.

Figures 2.3 and 2.4 show the number of papers submitted by the top eight countries: the US, the UK, Germany, Japan, France, Canada, Switzerland, and Australia. "High-impact journals" selected for the basic research were cell, nature medicine, nature immunology, and nature genetics. "High-impact journals" selected for

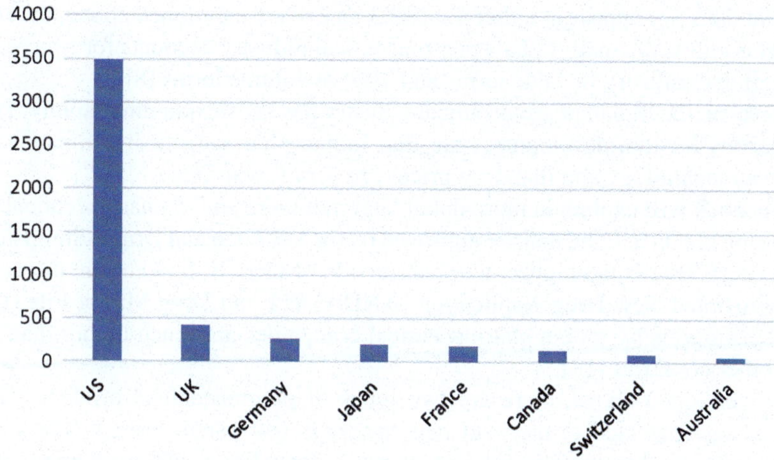

Fig. 2.3 Number of papers published in high-impact journals—basic medicines (*Source*: Office of Pharmaceutical Industry Research (OPIR), "Future Vision of the Pharmaceutical Industry: The Mission and Issues toward 2015" (Japan Pharmaceutical Manufacturers Association [JPMA], 2007): 118)

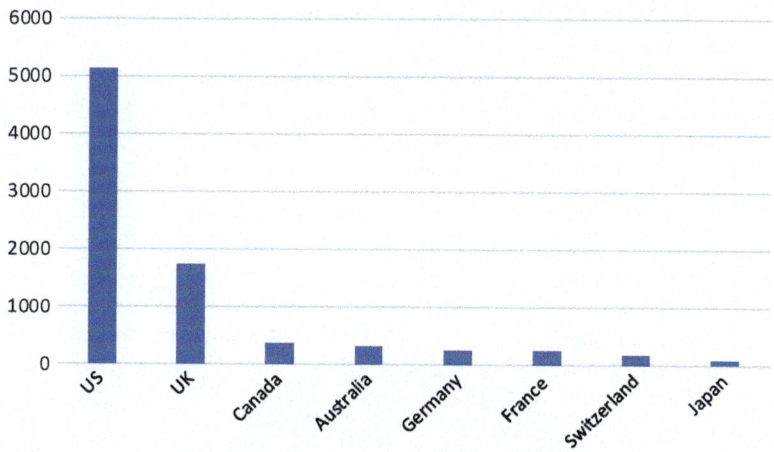

Fig. 2.4 Number of papers published in high-impact journals—clinical studies (*Source*: Office of Pharmaceutical Industry Research (OPIR), "Future Vision of the Pharmaceutical Industry: The Mission and Issues toward 2015" (Japan Pharmaceutical Manufacturers Association [JPMA], 2007): 118)

clinical studies/applied study research were the New England Journal of Medicine (NEJM), Lancet, and the Journal of the American Medical Association (JAMA). Japan was ranked No. 4 in basic medicine-related journals. On the other hand, Japan was the lowest-ranked among eight selected countries in clinical study/applied study journals [17].

India does not appear in either Table 2.3 or 2.4. As mentioned above, the Indian market is still very small: India's pharmaceutical industry accounts for a mere 2.4% of the global industry in value terms and 10% in volume terms [8].

However, the Indian pharmaceutical industry has been expanding rapidly. Two of the reasons for that development are that Indian pharmaceutical companies have advanced technology and that drug prices are very low in India.

This book will explain in more detail later, but there are 75 pharmaceutical manufacturing plants in India that are approved by the US Food and Drug Administration (FDA) #10. That is the highest number outside of the US. In addition, the number of Abbreviated New Drug Application (ANDA) #11 and Drug Master File (DMF) #12 registrations by Indian pharmaceutical companies are much higher than those from other countries [18].

As mentioned above, there are two types of pharmaceutical products: brand-name drugs (patented drugs) and generic drugs (off-patent drugs). The US and Europe are mixed markets featuring both types. Brand-name drugs are predominant in the Japanese market—but the proportion of generics has been increasing. Generic drugs dominate the Indian market.

Figure 2.5 is a conceptual figure showing the relative shares of brand-name drugs and generic drugs by country. The size of the circle/ellipse indicates market size. Generic drugs, as the name implies, are marketed under generic names. Those that offer little or no innovative value over the brand-name versions are sometimes called "plain vanilla generics."

Some generic drug makers are developing generic drugs (off-patent drugs) with added-value features—sustained release, user-friendliness, safety, etc.—and marketing them under brand names. These generics are called "branded generic drugs." Major Indian pharmaceutical companies, such as Dr. Reddy's, Lupin, Sun

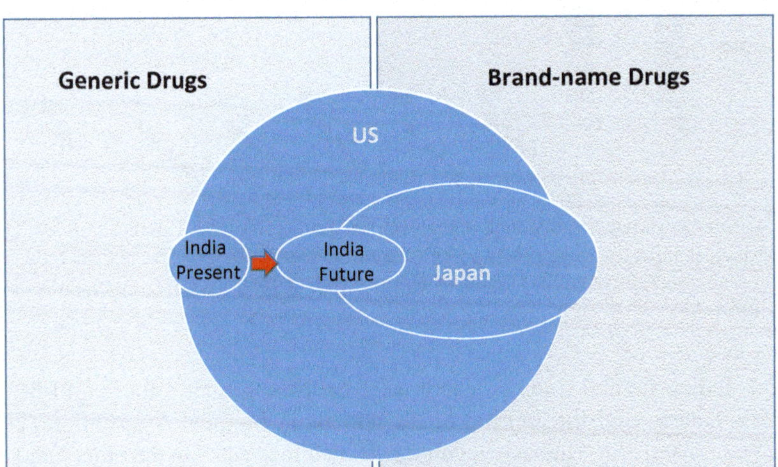

Fig. 2.5 Brand-name drugs vs. generic drugs

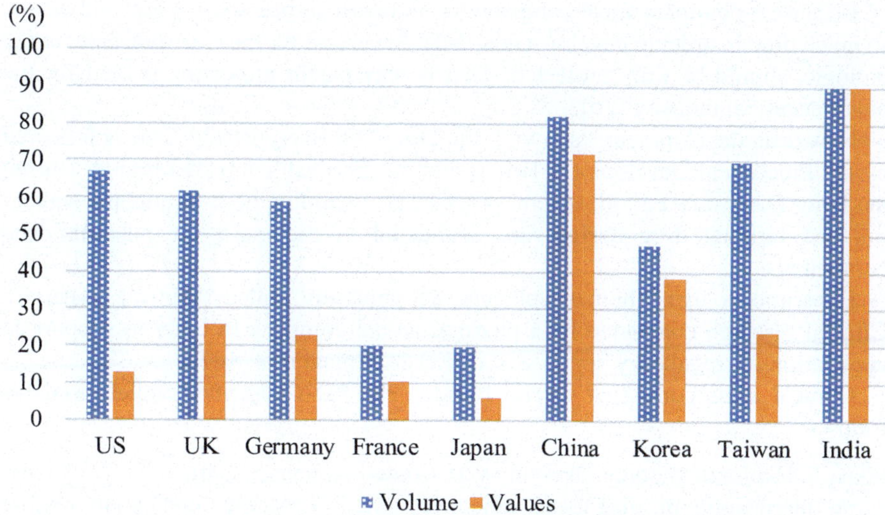

Fig. 2.6 Proportion of generic drugs by country 2007–2008 (*Source*: "The Current Status of the Indian Pharmaceutical Industry," (research materials, no. 400, The Japan Pharmaceutical Manufacturers Association [JPMA], July 2009): 8)

Pharmaceutical, and Cipla, are focusing on development and marketing of these branded generics and are expanding their sales [19, 20, 21, 22].

Figure 2.6 shows market shares of generic drugs in terms of both value and volume, by country. The generic drugs proportions in the graph are the market shares in each country's domestic market. Generic drugs account for 67% of the US market (by volume), and both the UK (62%) and Germany (59%) have high proportions of generics. However, the proportion is low in France (20.5%). In this graph, the Japanese generics proportion is 20% but it has been growing rapidly.

The generic drugs proportions are generally high in developing countries. In China, it is 82.2% and in India, it is 90%, according to the graph [23].

2.2 Remarkable Features of the Pharmaceutical Industry from the Perspective of Patent Protection

It takes a long time (10–15 years) and costs a huge amount of R&D investment money—as much as 10 billion yen—to develop a new drug. If failed projects are included, a new drug development cost could be 20–30 billion yen or even up to 50 billion yen in some cases [24].

It is said that, because the barriers to entry into a pharmaceutical market are extremely high, there are only seven countries in which new drugs are being developed: the US, the UK, Japan, France, Sweden, Germany, and Switzerland [25].

Because a pharmaceutical company has to invest so heavily in R&D and devote so much time in order to develop a new drug, the patent for the core molecule, or the biologic, should be fully protected. That is why patent protection is vital for the pharmaceutical industry [26].

New drug development starts with the Drug Discovery Period. This is followed by the Preclinical Development Period and the Clinical Trials #13 Period. During the Drug Discovery Period, several procedures, including high-throughput screening and rational drug design, are conducted in the quest for potential lead compounds.

Experiments using human subjects are generally called "clinical research." Clinical research conducted by a pharmaceutical company in order to support an application for regulatory approval is called a "clinical trial" [27].

Clinical trials consist of several phases. The FDA describes clinical trials as follows:

Phase 0: Exploratory study involving very limited human exposure to the drug, with no therapeutic or diagnostic objectives (e.g., screening studies, microdose studies).

Phase 1: Studies that are usually conducted with healthy volunteers and which are focused on safety. The objective is to identify what the drug's most frequent and serious adverse events are and, often, how the drug is metabolized and excreted.

Phase 2: Studies that gather preliminary data on effectiveness (whether or not the drug works in subjects who are suffering from a particular disease or medical condition). For example, participants receiving the drug may be compared to similar participants receiving a different treatment, usually an inactive substance called a placebo, or a different drug. Safety continues to be evaluated, and short-term adverse events are studied.

Phase 3: Studies that gather more information about safety and effectiveness by studying different populations and different dosages and by using the drug in combination with other drugs.

Phase 4: Studies occurring after the FDA has approved a drug for marketing. These include post-marketing requirements and commitment studies that are required of or agreed to by the study sponsor. These studies gather additional information about a drug's safety, efficacy, or optimal use [28, 29, 30].

NDA

After all three phases of clinical trials have been completed successfully, the pharmaceutical company must file a New Drug Application (NDA) #14 with a regulatory agency (in the case of the US, the FDA; in the case of European countries, the EMA). The pharmaceutical company must be able to clearly demonstrate the effectiveness and safety of the drug and must provide all of the scientific information that it has compiled on the specific drug.

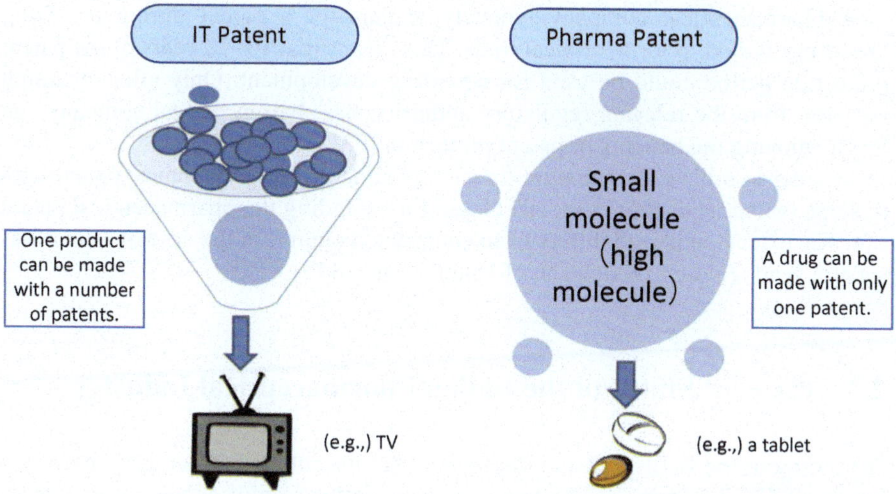

Fig. 2.7 Difference in roles of IP between consumer electronics industry and pharmaceutical industry

Approval

If the regulatory agency approves the drug, it is then made available for physicians to prescribe to patients. The pharmaceutical company is still responsible for submitting periodic reports to the regulatory agency [31].

The roles of patent protection differ from one industry to another. For instance, patent protection plays a different role in the IT/consumer electronics industry to that in the pharmaceutical industry [32]. In the consumer electronics industry, a company develops a product through dealing in thousands of licenses. This practice is called "cross-licensing" #15. But, in the pharmaceutical industry, a company may be able to develop one pharmaceutical product on the basis of a single product patent [32] (Fig. 2.7). Since pharmaceutical products directly impact human health, the producer of a drug has to obtain permission from a regulatory agency before the company begins marketing its product. The regulatory agencies for pharmaceutical products are the Ministry of Health, Labour and Welfare (MHLW) in Japan, the US Food and Drug Administration (FDA) in the US, and the European Medicines Agency (EMA) in Europe. A pharmaceutical company which wishes to market its pharmaceutical products must first pass through two barriers: patent application (to patent office) and approval by the regulatory agency.

One issue is that there are very longtime gaps between patent applications and new drug approvals. Under TRIPS, the patent protection period is set at 20 years from the date of patent application. As explained above, a pharmaceutical firm typically devotes between 10 and 20 years to discovering/developing a single drug [24].

A pharmaceutical company typically applies for a patent during the Drug Discovery Period, prior to clinical trials. This means that 10–20 years of the patent protection period could be used for new drug development. Only after obtaining approval from the relevant regulatory authority, the pharmaceutical company can begin enjoying the benefits of patent protection [33].

In order to relieve the situation for such pharmaceutical companies, patent laws in some countries contain a special clause for extending the pharmaceutical patent life. The extension period differs from country to country. In the case of Japan, it is set at 5 years. (Note 8: Extension of Patent Term) [34].

2.3 Current Status of the Indian Pharmaceutical Industry

According to the IBEF website, the Indian pharmaceutical market as of 2016 was worth US$36.7 billion. IBEF predicts that the industry will expand at an annual growth rate of 12.3% over the next 5 years, to reach US$55 billion [7] (Fig. 2.8). According to IBEF pharmaceuticals, the Indian pharmaceutical sector accounts for 2.4% of the global pharmaceutical industry in value terms and 10% in volume terms [8].

One notable feature of the Indian pharmaceutical industry is its export orientation. Indian pharmaceutical products are exported to more than 200 countries, with the US as the key market. As of 2016, India is the world's largest provider of generic drugs, with its products accounting for 20% of global generic drug exports (in terms of volume). In terms of value, exports of pharmaceutical products increased at an annual growth rate of around 14% between FY2012 and FY2015. During

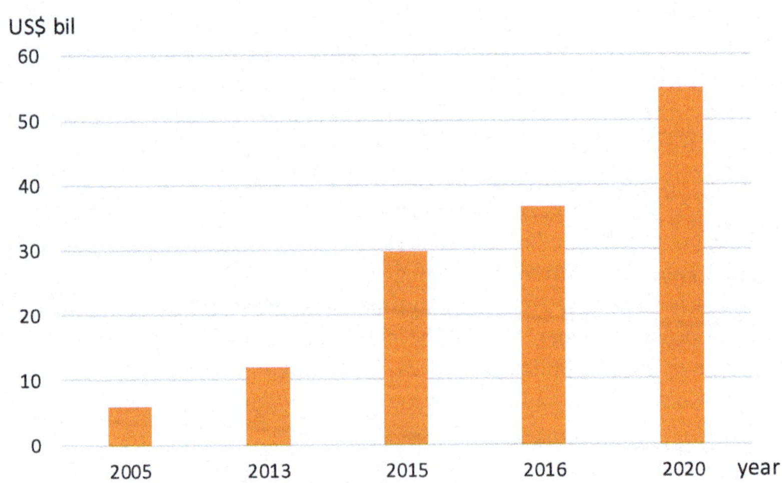

Fig. 2.8 Revenues of Indian pharmaceutical sector (*Source*: IBEF, Website (accessed June 2017))

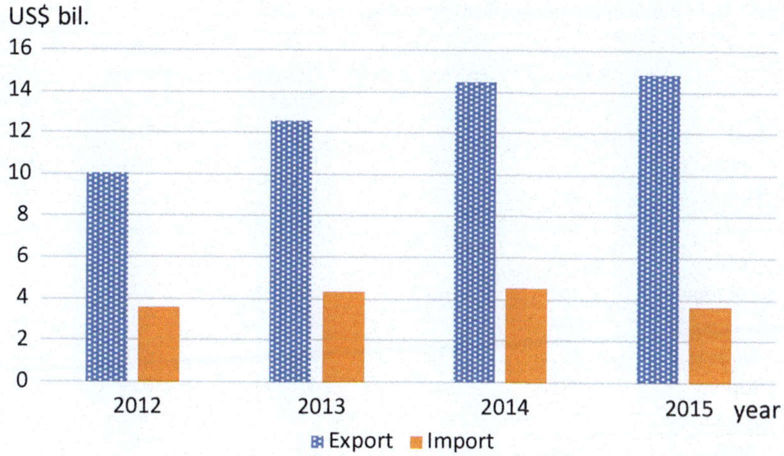

Fig. 2.9 Trade data of Indian pharma sector (*Source*: IBEF, "Pharmaceuticals" (Jan. 2017))

FY2012–2014, imports of pharmaceutical products rose at annual growth rate of 13.04% [35] (Fig. 2.9).

IBEF "pharmaceuticals," June 2017 describes the Indian pharmaceutical industry as having four main edges: (a) low cost, (b) economic growth, (c) diversified portfolio, and (d) government support [36].

A more detailed explanation follows:

(a) Low cost: India's cost of production is approximately 60% lower than that of the US and almost half that of Europe.
(b) Economic growth: India's economic prosperity has helped to improve drug affordability.
(c) Diversified portfolio: There are more than 60,000 generic brands across 60 therapeutic categories; Indian companies manufacture more than 500 different APIs.
(d) Government support: The Indian Government unveiled "Pharma Vision 2020," which is aimed at making India a global leader in end-to-end drug manufacturing [36].

According to the Indian Stock Online website, there are more than 20,000 pharmaceutical companies in India, and, together, the pharmaceutical industry and the IT/software industry have been maintaining strong international competitiveness and driving India's economy [37].

Leading pharmaceutical companies in India include Sun Pharmaceutical, Dr. Reddy's, Lupin, Cipla, Aurobindo, and Glenmark. Table 2.5 shows the top 10 Indian pharmaceutical companies as of 2015 [38].

Table 2.5 Top 10 Indian pharmaceutical companies as of 2015

		Revenues (mil $)	Domestic revenues (mil $)	Domestic ratio (%)	Foreign revenues (mil $)	Foreign ratio (%)
1	Sun	3,415	649	19	2,766	81
2	Dr. Reddy's	2,331	326	14	2,005	86
3	Lupin	1,981	476	24	1,505	76
4	Cipla	1,787	697	39	1,090	61
5	Cadila	1,346	417	31	929	69
6	Aurobindo	1,262	740	59	522	41
7	Glenmark	1,024	318	31	706	69
8	Jubilant	912	232	25	680	75
9	Torrent	728	299	41	429	59
10	Wockhardt	720	198	27.5	522	72.5
	Total	15,506	4,352	28	11,154	72

Source: "GMR Data: The Indian Pharmaceutical Market—Leading Domestic Companies" (2015): 46

2.3.1 *Indian Pharmaceutical Companies vs. Foreign Pharmaceutical Companies*

As mentioned above, in the wake of enforcement of the Indian Patents Act, 1970, foreign-owned companies which were not happy about operating in a market without patent protection withdrew one after another from the Indian market.

The only exception was GSK, which remained in India and achieved a certain degree of success in the domestic market without the benefit of patent protection. Hasit Joshipura, GSK's Senior Vice President, South Asia & Managing Director, India, interviewed by the author of this study, said that GSK remained in India because it is a UK company [39].

Following India's introduction of product patents in 2005, foreign-owned pharmaceutical companies gradually re-entered the Indian market. The "Asia Business Generator Project: Overview of Indian Pharmaceutical Industry" report compiled by Tata Strategic Management Group in 2008 noted that domestic pharmaceutical firms commanded 95% of the Indian market [40].

2.3.2 *Disease Profile in India*

According to "Asia Business Generator Project: Overview of Indian Pharmaceutical Industry," compiled by Tata Strategic Management Group, approximately 70% of the pharmaceutical products sold in India are for treating acute diseases #16, and the other 30% are for treating chronic diseases #17 [41].

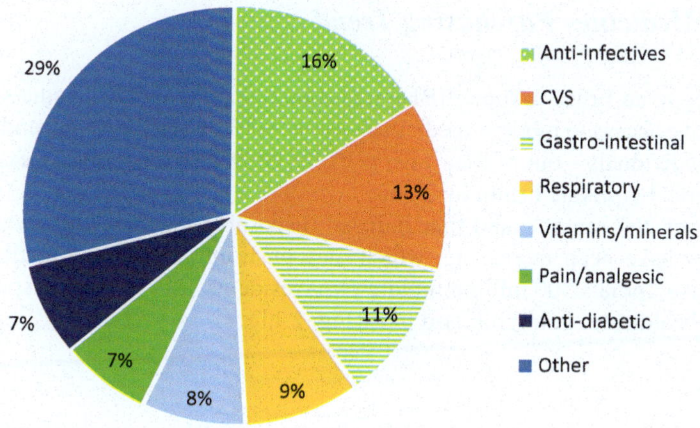

Fig. 2.10 Indian pharmaceutical sales by Disease Profile FY2015 (*Source*: Umesh Chandra et al. Ref. [42])

Figure 2.10 shows Indian pharmaceutical sales by Disease Profile for FY2015. In FY2015, anti-infective drugs held the largest share (16%) of total sales of pharmaceutical products in India. Sales of cardiovascular products stood at 13% and anti-diabetic drugs at 7%. The growing number of patients suffering from lifestyle-related medical conditions in India looks likely to contribute to increasing sales in these two categories in the coming years.

According to "Diet in an Aging Society, Diabetes," there are more than 40 million diabetes patients in India, the highest number in the world, and that figure is expected to further increase [42, 43].

2.3.3 Regulation of Drugs in India

According to "Asia Business Generator Project: Overview of Indian Pharmaceutical Industry," compiled by Tata Strategic Management Group, the Indian government regulates intellectual property, price, and quality of pharmaceutical products [44].

The Drugs and Cosmetics Act, 1940 is an Act of the Parliament of India that regulates the importation, manufacture, and distribution of drugs in India [45].

In India, the Drugs Prices Control Order (DPCO) 1995 caps prices for essential drugs. Under DPCO 1995, 74 essential drug prices were controlled. The Indian government issued a new DPCO, DPCO 2013, on May 15, 2013. Under this new order, a total 348 new drug prices are controlled [46].

2.3.4 *Medicines Purchasing Trend*

According to an Ernst & Young/IBEF report in 2006, only 30% of India's 1 billion people have access to modern medicines. About 80% of healthcare expenditure was paid by individuals—out of their own pockets. Only 3% of healthcare expenditure was covered by private health insurance.

However, the report noted that Indians' disposable incomes and awareness of medicines have been increasing, which may push up healthcare spending in the future. Also, India's 300 million middle-class residents are expected to spend much more on healthcare, going forward [47] (Fig. 2.11).

2.3.5 *Advanced Technology in the Indian Pharmaceutical Industry*

As mentioned, one notable feature of the Indian pharmaceutical industry is its export orientation. Nearly half of all pharmaceutical products made in India are exported. The US is the leading destination for Indian pharmaceutical products (as of 2016).

According to Kazuki Minato, the US is the world's most stringently regulated pharmaceutical products market. There are high barriers to entry. The fact that India is exporting pharmaceutical products to the US market in large volumes is testament to the Indian pharmaceutical industry's advanced technological capabilities [48].

For the same reason, India has the largest number of FDA-approved drug manufacturing plants. According to the PricewaterhouseCoopers report "Global Pharma Looks to India: Prospects for Growth," the US FDA has approved more than 100 Indian manufacturing sites—more than in any country outside of the US [49] (Fig. 2.12).

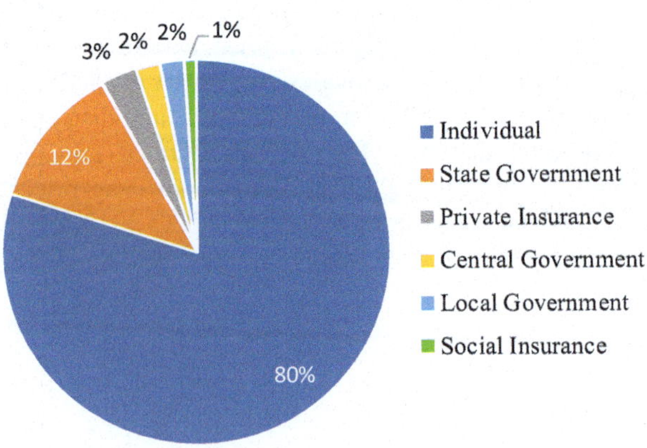

Fig. 2.11 Breakdown of healthcare expenditure (*Source*: Ernst & Young/ IBEF, "Pharmaceuticals" (2006): 3)

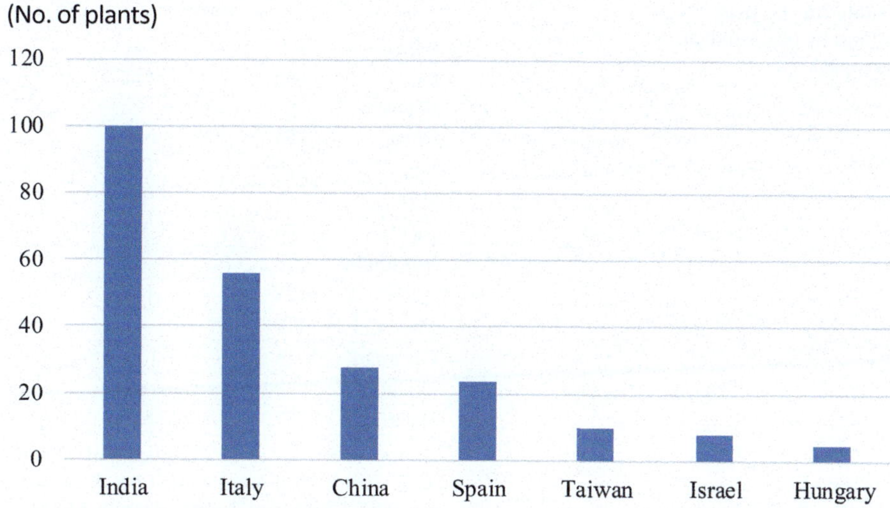

Fig. 2.12 FDA-approved manufacturing plants

Furthermore, the numbers of Drug Master Files (DMFs) applications and Abbreviated New Drug Applications (ANDAs) from Indian pharmaceutical companies made to the FDA have been growing rapidly.

According to Y. Srihari et al., Indian pharmaceutical companies started filing DMFs in the US in the 1980s. But, until the late 1990s, only a few DMFs had been filed. The proportion of total DMFs filed with the FDA from India has increased from 18.3% in 2001 to 44% in 2006. By 2006, India had become the leader in filing DMFs, with a total 738 filed to that point. As of March 2009, Dr. Reddy's, Cipla, Sun, and Aurobindo had each filed more than 100 DMFs.

Indian companies have also been filing a large number of ANDAs. Until recently, only a few had filed ANDAs; however, the situation has changed drastically. According to Srihari et al., the number of ANDA filings by the top 12 companies as of March 2009 had reached 1129 [50] (Table 2.6).

2.3.6 *Development of the Indian Pharmaceutical Industry*

Although India has long been known for its strengths in chemistry, the Indian pharmaceutical industry has only achieved rapid development since the 1970s. Before that, it was small in scale. As previously noted, the Indian pharmaceutical market was dominated by foreign-owned companies until the Patents Act, 1970 was enforced [51].

Under the Patents Act, 1970, which did not contain any product patent protection clauses, Indian companies could "legally" reverse engineer brand-name drugs (patented drugs), create new processes, manufacture copies of brand-name drugs, and market them as "generic" drugs [52].

Table 2.6 DMF & ANDA filings by major Indian companies

Company	No. of DMFs	No. of ANDAs
Ranbaxy	107	241
Dr. Reddy's	160	144
Cipla	153	NA
Sun	129	179
Lupin	85	90
Cadila	76	92
Wockhardt	66	67
Aurobindo	128	147
Matrix	115	41
Glenmark	45	71
Orchid	73	57
Hetero	57	NA

Source: Y. Srihari et al. "Implications of Drug Price Competition and Patent Term Restoration Act (DPCPTRA) on Indian Pharma Industry," *Journal of Intellectual Property Rights* 14 (Nov. 2009): 502–503

As mentioned above, foreign-owned companies, unhappy with the lack of product patent protection, withdrew one after another from the Indian market. Meanwhile, Indian pharmaceutical companies were successfully expanding their businesses by employing an exclusively generic drugs business model based on reverse engineering technology. Eventually, Indian pharmaceutical companies came to dominate the domestic market [53].

After almost all of the foreign-owned companies had moved out of India, entry barriers to the Indian pharmaceutical market were virtually eliminated. In due course, a large number of companies came into the market and competition among them became increasingly fierce, pushing down domestic drug prices. According to Minato, drug prices in India were the lowest in the world [54].

Then, the Indian government introduced a price control scheme for essential medicines, which further lowered drug prices.

Lower prices gave Indian pharmaceutical products a strong competitive edge. The combination of very low prices and high quality won popularity for Indian products not only at home but also in overseas markets. Exports of both Indian bulk/intermediates and formulations expanded rapidly [55].

Initially, Indian pharmaceutical companies exported their products to Russia and so-called "Third World" countries such as certain Asian and African countries. However, as India gained in technological advancement, Indian pharmaceutical companies began exporting their products to the regulated markets, including the US. As of 2016, the US market is the main destination for Indian pharmaceutical products [56].

Further, using the earnings from their successful export operations, major Indian pharmaceutical companies acquired companies, mainly generic drug manufacturers, in other countries. Utilizing these acquired overseas businesses, those leading Indian companies set up sales and R&D channels outside of India. Imports of raw materials expanded rapidly, but imports of formulations increased only slightly [57].

2.4 Indian Patent Law

2.4.1 Transition of Indian Patent Law

India has a long history of patent protection. In 1856, while still a British colony, India enacted a law for granting exclusive privileges to creators of outstanding and novel inventions. In 1911, the Patents and Designs Act, 1911 was enacted [58].

Under the Patents and Designs Act, 1911, both product and process were protected. The period of protection was set at a minimum of 16 years.

As mentioned above (Sect. 1.2.2), the Indian government drastically revised its patent law in 1970. The Indian Patents Act, 1970 came into force in 1972 [59].

Under the Indian Patents Act, 1970, product patents for new chemical entities (NCEs) were not protected; only process patents were protected.

In addition, the protection period for process patents was determined to be the shorter of either 5 years from approval or 7 years from patent application. However, as mentioned above, due to enforcement of TRIPS, India was required to revise the Patents Act, 1970 into an international patent law or a TRIPS-compatible law.

TRIPS granted a 5-year grace period for developing countries to revise their patent systems and employ TRIPS-compatible patents. In addition, TRIPS granted another 5-year grace period for countries that did not have any product patents in 1995.

India was deemed to be a developing country and did not have any product patents in 1995. That is why India was granted a total 10-year grace period and was required to revise its patent system and introduce product patents by January 1, 2005 [60].

In order to meet its obligations under TRIPS, India revised its patent law through a three-stage process. First, in 1999, India instituted the "mailbox" (Note 9: Mailbox) requirement of TRIPS Article 70.8, which enabled pharmaceutical companies and chemical companies to submit product patent applications for pharmaceuticals and agricultural chemicals to the patent office that would be held until examination in 2005. Also, in accordance with TRIPS Article 70.9, India set up an EMR framework, which grants the applicant (if approved) exclusive marketing rights (EMR) for 5 years (Note 10: EMR) [61].

Second, India introduced the Patents (Amendment) Act, 2002, which further integrated Indian law by extending the patent term to 20 years, as stipulated in TRIPS Article 33 (Note 11: Term of Protection) [62].

India was planning to introduce product patents by applying a third revision to the Patents Act by January 2005; however, it appeared that the revision bill would not pass through the Indian parliament in time to meet the deadline of January 1. In order to meet the deadline, the Indian government passed a Presidential

Ordinance for Revising the Act on December 26, 2004, and formally passed a revision bill and introduced a pro forma revised patent law on January 1, 2005. The actual revision bill for the Act went through Parliament in March, and the President signed the bill on April 4, 2005. The revision act was enforced retroactively, as of January 1, 2005 [63].

India's Patents (Amendment) Act, 2005 was deemed to be an international patent law or a TRIPS-compatible patent law. However, the Indian government inserted a special clause called Section 3 (d), which restricts the scope of patentability [64].

In fact, the Indian Patent Office rejected many patent applications on the basis of Section 3 (d). One of the best known cases was that involving the major Swiss pharmaceutical company, Novartis, whose Gleevec patent was rejected by the Indian Patent Office. Gleevec, a blockbuster anti-cancer drug, had been granted patents in more than 40 countries. When Novartis' patent application was rejected in India, the issue received heavy international press coverage [65].

2.4.2 *Section 3 (d) of Patents (Amendment) Act, 2005 of India*

As mentioned above, the Patents (Amendment) Act, 2005 of India contains a unique clause called Section 3 (d), which restricts patentability.

Section 3 (d) is shown below.

Section 3 (d): The mere discovery of a new form of a known substance which does not result in the enhancement of the known efficacy of that substance or the mere discovery of any new property or new use for a known substance or of the mere new use of a known process, machine, or apparatus unless such known process results in a new product or employs at least one new reactant.

Explanation: For the purposes of this clause, salts, esters, ethers, polymorphs, metabolites, pure form, particle size, isomers, mixtures of isomers, complexes, combinations, and other derivatives of a known substance shall be considered to be the same substance, unless they differ significantly in properties with regard to efficacy.

Section 3 (d) mentions that it will admit patentability when the molecule (the subject of the patent application) is an NCE, without argument. However, if the molecule is a known substance, it will admit patentability only when it shows enhancement of the known efficacy. The section does not mention what kind/type of efficacy is meant [66].

When Novartis' Gleevec patent application was rejected by the Indian Patent Office on the basis of Section 3 (d), Novartis took the case to court [65].

The Madras High Court and IPAB, which dealt with the Gleevec case, argued that "efficacy" in Section 3 (d) means therapeutic efficacy. However, as mentioned above, a pharmaceutical company tends to submit a patent application during the Drug Discovery Period, whereas therapeutic efficacy data is only compiled and available after completion of clinical trials. That is why it is quite difficult for a pharmaceutical company to demonstrate therapeutic efficacy at the stage of submitting a patent application [67, 68].

2.4.3 Mailbox

TRIPS granted a 5-year grace period for developing countries to revise their patent systems and employ TRIPS-compatible patents. In addition, TRIPS granted another 5-year grace period for countries that did not have any product patents in 1995 [60].

On the other hand, TRIPS required all member countries that were granted grace periods to set up a "mailbox," which enabled pharmaceutical companies and chemical companies to submit product patent applications for pharmaceuticals and agricultural chemicals to the patent office that would be held until examination in 2005 [60].

India, in its revision act of 1999, set up a "mailbox" to meet the requirement of TRIPS Article 70.8, and the system took effect, retroactively, as of 1995 [61].

According to the Indian Patent Office, the IPO had received 7,945 pharmaceutical-related patent applications as of December 31, 2004. Of those, the IPO had granted patents in respect of 1,876 applications as of October 2008 [69] (Table 2.7).

2.4.4 EMR

TRIPS also required all member countries to introduce an EMR framework which grants the patent applicant (if its patent application is approved) exclusive marketing rights (EMR) for 5 years. In order to meet the TRIPS requirement, India introduced EMR in The Patents (Amendment) Act, 1999 [61].

According to the Indian Patent Office, the IPO has received 14 applications for EMR. Among them, four applications were granted EMR [70] (Table 2.8).

Table 2.7 Mailbox applications and patents granted

	No. of mail box applications			Patents granted (up to Oct. 31, 2008)		
Type	Indian applications	Foreign applications	Total	Indian	Foreign	Total
Pharmaceuticals	1,313	6,632	7,945	260	1,616	1,876
Agrochemicals	146	827	973	23	176	199
Total	1,459	7,459	8,918	283	1,792	2,075

Source: IPO 2009

Table 2.8 Applications for and grants of EMR

SL No.	Application number	Date of application	Applicant	Corresponding patent	Name of product	Activity of product	Status of EMR
1	EMR/1/2000	Feb. 24, 2000	F. Hoffmann La Roche AG Switzerland	910/Mas/96, Dated May 28, 1996	Saquinavir mesylate equivalent to Saquinavir 200 mg Capsule	Selective HIV proteinase Inhibitor	Refused. Refusal challenged in the HC, Kolkata, status of the case: pending
2	EMR/2/2000	Jun. 30, 2000	SmithKline Beecham PLC, UK	2504/Del/98 Dated Aug. 25,1998	Rosiglitazone maleate tablet equivalent to 1 mg/2 mg/4 mg/8 mg Rosiglitazone	Antidiabetic	Refused
3	EMR/3/2000	Jun. 30, 2000	SmithKline Beecham PLC, UK	2505/del/98 Dated Aug. 25, 1998	Rosiglitazone maleate tablet equivalent to 1 mg/2 mg/4 mg/8 mg rosiglitazone	Antidiabetic	Refused
4	EMR/1/2001	Jun. 26, 2001	Bayer Aktiengesellschaft, Germany	315/Del/2000 Dated March 27, 2000 Antedated to Dec. 6,1996 Divided out of 2723/Del/96 (185805)	Moxifloxacin Hydrochloride and moxifloxacin Hydrochloride tablet equivalent to moxifloxacin 400 mg	Antidiabetic	Pending
5	EMR/2/20/1	Aug. 07, 2001	United Phosphorus Ltd. Gujarat, India	570/Mum/2000 Dated June 21, 2000	Synergistic Fungicidal Composition Comprising Carbendazim and mancozeb	Antifungal Insecticide	Granted Sept 5, 2003. The EMR terminated with effect from Jan 12, 2007 notified OJ, Issue No. 11/2007 dated March 16, 2007

6	EMR/3/20/01	Aug. 30, 2001	Schering-Plough Corporation, US	IN/PCT/2000/0 0434/CHC Sept. 2, 2000	PEG Interferon-alpha Conjugates	Anticancer	Pending
7	EMR/4/20/01	Oct. 10, 2001	Ranbaxy Laboratories, Ltd., New Delhi	2660/del/97	Ciprofloxacine	Antibiotic	Refused
				2745/del/98	Composition		
8	EMR/1/20/02	Mar. 26, 2002	Novartis AG, Switzerland	1602/MAS/98	Imatinib mesylate	Chronic myeloid leukemia (CML) antitumor agent	Granted Nov. 10, 2003
9	EMR/1/20/03	Jul. 17, 2003	Wockhardt Ltd., Bandra Wockhardt Tower, Bandra Kurla Complex, Bandra (East) Mumbai 400,051	308/MUM/2002 March 28, 2002	Nadifloxacin 1% cream	Antibacterial	Granted Dec 15, 2003, Writ petition no. 802 of 2005 pending in Mumbai HC EMR terminated with effect from May 18, 2006 Notification issued OJ 31/2006 dated Magu 4, 2006
10	EMR/2/20/03	Oct. 16, 2003	Nicholas Piramal India Limited, Mumbai 400,012 and Council of Scientific and Industrial Research New Delhi 110,001	501/MUM/2000 May 31, 2000	Bulaquine Capsule	Antimalarial	Pending

(continued)

Table 2.8 (continued)

SL No.	Application number	Date of application	Applicant	Corresponding patent	Name of product	Activity of product	Status of EMR
11	EMR/3/20/03	Oct. 10, 2003	Eli Lilly Company US	85/DEL/1995 Jan. 23, 1995	Tadalafil tablet	Erectile Dysfunction	Granted Aug 26, 2004 Grant challenged in the HC, Kolkata. Grant stayed
12	EMR/1/20/04	Mar. 01, 2003	F. Hoffmann La Roche AG Switzerland	1032/MAS/97 May 15, 2007	Interferon Conjugates	Anticancer	Pending
13	EMR/2/20/04	Jun. 14, 2004	Panacea Biotech Lot, India	2047/Del/95 Nov. 08, 1995 (Process patent granted 2048/Del/95)	Nimesulide inj.	Analgesic	Pending
14	EMR/3/20/04	Sep. 13, 2004	Panacea Biotech Lot, India	57/Del/98 Jan. 12, 1998	Nimesulide inj.	Analgesic	Pending

Source: Indian Patent Office 2009

References

1. Kohei Shiino, *Basic Data on the Indian Economy: The Current Status and Policies of the New Economic Giant* (JETRO, 2009), 8.
2. World Bank, "Global Economic Prospects, June 2016: Divergences and Risks" (June 2016).
3. Gulshan Akhtar, "Indian Pharmaceutical Industry: An Overview," *IOSR Journal of Humanities and Social Science* 13, no. 3 (Jul.-Aug. 2013): 65.
4. Takashi Kadokura, "Indian Pharmaceutical Industry Standing on a Turning Point," *Asia Trends* (Dai-ichi Life Research Institute, June 2005): 1.
5. Koji Takeda, "The Indian Pharmaceutical Industry, along with IT, Is Targeting the World Market," Chap. 74 in *The Book of Indian IT* (Nihon Keizai Shimbun, 2009).
6. *OECD Health Policy Studies: Pharmaceutical Pricing Policies in a Global Market* (OECD Publishing, 2008), 58.
7. IBEF Website, https://www.ibef.org/industry/pharmaceutical-india.aspx (accessed June 2017).
8. IBEF Pharmaceuticals (June 2017): 3. https://www.ibef.org/industry/indian-pharmaceuticals-industry-analysis-presentation.
9. Toshimitsu Kurogi, "Strengths and Weaknesses of Indian Pharmaceutical Companies," Chap. 14 in *The Current Status of Indian Pharmaceutical Industry* (Yakuji Nippo, Yakuji Nippo Limited, Sept. 2007).
10. William Greene, "The Emergence of India's Pharmaceutical Industry and Implications for the U.S. Generic Drug Market" (Office of Economics working paper, no. 2007-05-A, U.S. International Trade Commission, May 2007): 16.
11. Office of Pharmaceutical Industry Research (OPIR), "Future Vision of the Pharmaceutical Industry: The Mission and Issues toward 2015" (Japan Pharmaceutical Manufacturers Association [JPMA], 2007): 146.
12. Japan Generic Medicines Association (news release, Sept. 29, 2016).
13. IBEF, "Pharmaceuticals" (June. 2017): 11.
14. Office of Pharmaceutical Industry Research (OPIR), "Current Status of and Issues Surrounding the Pharmaceutical Industry: In Order to Provide Better Medicines" (Japan Pharmaceutical Manufacturers Association [JPMA], 2015): 16.
15. Office of Pharmaceutical Industry Research (OPIR), "Current Status of and Issues Surrounding the Pharmaceutical Industry: In Order to Provide Better Medicines" (Japan Pharmaceutical Manufacturers Association [JPMA], 2015): 17.
16. Office of Pharmaceutical Industry Research (OPIR), "Future Vision of the Pharmaceutical Industry: The Mission and Issues toward 2015" (Japan Pharmaceutical Manufacturers Association [JPMA], 2007): 178.
17. Office of Pharmaceutical Industry Research (OPIR), "Future Vision of the Pharmaceutical Industry: The Mission and Issues toward 2015" (Japan Pharmaceutical Manufacturers Association [JPMA], 2007): 118.
18. Tata Strategic Management Group, "Asia Business Generator Project: Overview of the Indian Pharmaceutical Industry" (March 2008): 2.
19. Dr. Reddy's, "Annual Report," http://www.drreddys.com/investors/reports-and-filings/annual-reports/.
20. Lupin, "Annual Report," http://www.lupinworld.com/archives-annual-report.htm.
21. Sun Pharma, "Annual Report," http://www.sunpharma.com/investors/annualreports.
22. Cipla, "Annual Report," http://www.cipla.com/en/investor-information/financial-results.html.
23. "The Current Status of the Indian Pharmaceutical Industry" (research materials, no. 400, The Japan Pharmaceutical Manufacturers Association [JPMA], July 2009): 8.
24. Kuwashima K. Management of Uncertainty: Solution for Pharmaceutical R&D Management. *Nikkei BP*. 2006;22
25. Office of Pharmaceutical Industry Research (OPIR), "Toward Strengthening Competitive Power in the Field of Drug Development: The Current Status and Issues of the Pharmaceutical Industry" (Japan Pharmaceutical Manufacturers Association [JPMA], Nov. 2005): 4.

26. Hiroyuki Odagiri, *Economics of Biotechnology* (Toyo Keizai Inc., 2006), 121.
27. Ministry of Health, Labour and Welfare Website, http://www.mhlw.go.jp/stf/seisakunitsuite/bunya/fukyu1.html.
28. ClinicalTrials.gov, "A Service of the U.S. National Institutes of Health: Glossary of Common Site Terms," https://clinicaltrials.gov/ct2/about-studies/glossary#P.
29. FDA, "FDA Special Consumer Report: Inside Clinical Trials – Testing Medical Products in People," http://www.fda.gov/Drugs/ResourcesForYou/Consumers/ucm143531.htm.
30. FDA, "FDA Special Consumer Report: The Beginnings – Laboratory and Animal Studies," http://www.fda.gov/Drugs/ResourcesForYou/Consumers/ucm143475.htm.
31. The Japan Pharmaceutical Manufacturers Association (JPMA), Clinical Trial Ruling,http://www.jpma.or.jp/medicine/shinyaku/chiken_02.html.
32. Hiroshi Akimoto, "R&D Strategy of the Japanese Pharmaceutical Industry and Bio Technology" (presentation material, Path of Bio Innovation and Future Development, Industry-Academy-Govt. Collaboration Workshop, Roppongi Hills, March 10, 2009): 43.
33. Clinical Trial Navi Website, "Patent Term Extension," http://www.chikennavi.net/word/tokkyokikan.htm.
34. *Japanese Patent Act [Art. 67 (2)]*, Ministry of Justice Website, http://www.japaneselawtranslation.go.jp/law/detail/?printID=&ft=1&co=01&x=32&y=19&ky=%E7%89%B9%E8%A8%B1%E6%B3%95&page=10&id=42&lvm=&re=02&vm=02.
35. IBEF, "Pharmaceuticals" (June. 2017): 13.
36. IBEF, "Pharmaceuticals" (Jan. 2017): 5.
37. Indian Stock Online Website, "Indian Pharmaceutical Industry," http://www.indokeizai.com/industry/medicine.html.
38. "GMR Data: The Indian Pharmaceutical Market – Leading Domestic Companies" (2015): 46.
39. Hasit Joshipura (senior vice president, South Asia & Managing Director – India, GSK), interview on July 23, 2009.
40. Tata Strategic Management Group, "Asia Business Generator Project: Overview of the Indian Pharmaceutical Industry" (March 2008): 1.
41. Tata Strategic Management Group, "Asia Business Generator Project: Overview of the Indian Pharmaceutical Industry" (March 2008): 4.
42. Umesh Chandra et al., "Opportunities and Challenges of Indian Pharmaceutical Sector: An Overview," *International Journal of Scientific Research and Management (IJSRM)* 4, no. 6 (2016): 4293.
43. "Diet in an Aging Society, Diabetes," *Global by Nippon Suisan Kaisha, Ltd.*, no. 57 (Aug. 2007): 1, http://www.nissui.co.jp/news/20070828.html.
44. Tata Strategic Management Group, "Asia Business Generator Project: Overview of the Indian Pharmaceutical Industry" (March 2008): 4.
45. *The Drugs and Cosmetics Act, 1940, Act No. 23 of 1940* (April 10, 1940), with 2005 amendments., http://www.prsindia.org/uploads/media/1188536330/bill145_20080430145_THE_DRUGS_AND_COSMETICS_ACT_1940_with_2005_amendments.pdf.
46. *Drugs (Prices Control) Order, 2013*, Ministry of Chemicals and Fertilizers (May 15, 2013), http://www.nppaindia.nic.in/DPCO2013.pdf.
47. Ernst & Young/IBEF, "Pharmaceuticals" (2006): 3.
48. Kazuki Minato, "Indian Pharmaceutical Industry – Structural Background for Development and Changes after TRIPS," *Japanese Generic Medicine Market and Indian & Chinese Pharmaceutical Industries*, ed. Kensuke Kubo (Institute of Developing Economies-JETRO, 2007), 24.
49. PricewaterhouseCoopers, "Global Pharma Looks to India: Prospects for Growth" (2010): 12.
50. Y. Srihari et al., "Implications of Drug Price Competition and Patent Term Restoration Act (DPCPTRA) on Indian Pharma Industry," *Journal of Intellectual Property Rights* 14 (Nov. 2009): 502–503.
51. Kazuki Minato, "Indian Pharmaceutical Industry – Structural Background for Development and Changes after TRIPS," *Japanese Generic Medicine Market and Indian & Chinese*

Pharmaceutical Industries, ed. Kensuke Kubo (Institute of Developing Economies-JETRO, 2007), 31.

52. Atsuko Kamiike et al., "Production Dynamics in Indian Pharmaceutical Industry: Utilizing Individual Data from the Annual Census of Manufacture" (discussion paper, Research Institute of Kobe University, June 21, 2011): 1–37.
53. Kazuki Minato, "Indian Pharmaceutical Industry – Structural Background for Development and Changes after TRIPS," *Japanese Generic Medicine Market and Indian & Chinese Pharmaceutical Industries*, ed. Kensuke Kubo (Institute of Developing Economies-JETRO, 2007), 33.
54. Kazuki Minato, "Indian Pharmaceutical Industry – Structural Background for Development and Changes after TRIPS," *Japanese Generic Medicine Market and Indian & Chinese Pharmaceutical Industries*, ed. Kensuke Kubo (Institute of Developing Economies-JETRO, 2007), 34–35.
55. Toru Noji, "Current Status of the Indian Pharmaceutical Industry: The Market, Company Trends, Strategies for Dealing with Changes in the Environment," *Mizuho Industry Focus* 51 (Industry Research Division, Mizuho Corporate Bank, Nov. 2, 2006): 6.
56. Kazuhiro Kawabata, "Overseas Penetration by Indian Pharmaceutical Companies," Chap. 15 in *The Current Status of Indian Pharmaceutical Industry* (Yakuji Nippo, Yakuji Nippo Limited, Sept. 11, 2007).
57. R. Joseph, "India's Trade in Drugs and Pharmaceuticals: Emerging Trends, Opportunities and Challenges" (RIS discussion paper, no. 159, Nov. 2009): 1–45.
58. Indian Patent Office Website, *The Indian Patents and Designs Act, 1911*., http://www.theindianlawyer.in/statutesnbareacts/acts/d42.html.
59. Indian Patent Office Website, *IP Act and Rules*, http://www.ipindia.nic.in/history-of-indian-patent-system.htm.
60. WTO Website, "Transitional Arrangements," http://www.wto.org/english/docs_e/legal_e/27-trips_08_e.htm.
61. WIPO Website in India, *The Patents (Amendment) Act, 1999*., http://www.wipo.int/wipolex/en/details.jsp?id=7622.
62. WTO Website in India, *The Patents (Amendment) Act, 2002*, http://www.wipo.int/wipolex/en/details.jsp?id=7620.
63. WIPO Website, *Patents (Amendment) Act, 2005 (Act No. 15 of 2005)*, http://www.wipo.int/edocs/lexdocs/laws/en/in/in065en.pdf.
64. Keiji Iwata, "The Effect of the Indian Patent Law Amendment," *Patent* 61, no. 2 (Feb. 2008): 44.
65. Mika Yamana, "Pharmaceutical Industry and the Indian Patent Act with Particular Reference to Madras High Court's Novartis Rulings," *Patent Studies*, no. 44 (Sept. 2007): 37.
66. WIPO Website, *Patents (Amendment) Act, 2005 (Act No. 15 of 2005)*, http://www.wipo.int/edocs/lexdocs/laws/en/in/in065en.pdf.
67. *Madras High Court Judgement,* http://www.lawyerscollective.org/files/novartis/IIMadHC/Novartis%20AG%20v%20UoI%20and%20others%20[Mad%20HC%20judgment].pdf.
68. IPAB Order Dated 26-Jun-2009 in Novartis v. Union of India https://ja.scribd.com/document/133340456/IPAB-Order-Dated-26-Jun-2009-in-Novartis-v-Union-of-India
69. Data directly obtained by the author during a visit to the Indian Patent Office (2009).
70. Data directly obtained by the author during a visit to the Indian Patent Office (2009).

Chapter 3
Research Subject and Methodology

This chapter describes the hypothesis of this study and the research methodology adopted. First, it explains the background to the research subject. Then, it covers the setting up of a hypothesis. It moves on to describe the research framework by way of a conceptual figure. To prove the hypothesis, this study conducts a two-phase analysis: Phase I analyzes "the Roles of the Indian Pharmaceutical Industry" and Phase II analyzes "the Roles of the Indian Government."

3.1 Setting up a Hypothesis

The pharmaceutical industry in India, which is categorized as a developing country, has been achieving healthy development, even after the introduction of product patents in 2005 and despite evidence in some earlier literature (Note: details are shown in Chap. 4) that pharmaceutical industries in developing countries tend to decline following introduction of product patent regimes.

The Indian government inserted Section 3 (d) into the Patents (Amendment) Act, 2005 in order to make it possible to meet the TRIPS commitments while also protecting the Indian pharmaceutical industry against market incursions by foreign-owned companies. Section 3 (d) could be a reason for the healthy development of the Indian pharmaceutical industry even after 2005. This study set up a hypothesis in order to clarify the part played by Section 3 (d).

Y. Mitsumori, *The Indian Pharmaceutical Industry*,
SpringerBriefs in Health Care Management and Economics,
https://doi.org/10.1007/978-981-10-6790-7_3

3.2 Hypothesis

This study set up the following hypothesis:

Section 3 (d), inserted into the Patents (Amendment) Act, 2005 by the Indian government, served to mitigate the negative impact that introduction of product patents would normally have on a country's economy.

If this hypothesis is proved, this study will conclude that the following is verified: Insertion of Section 3 (d) into the Patents (Amendment) Act, 2005 mitigated the negative impact of product patents in India and had a positive effect on development of the Indian pharmaceutical industry.

3.3 Research Subject and Methodology

This study is aimed at analyzing the impact of public policy (Patent Law) on industries (in this case, the pharmaceutical industry). In examining the impact of public policy on industries, two actors should be considered: one actor is industry (in this case, the Indian pharmaceutical industry); the other is government, which formulates policies (in this case, the Indian government). Thus, in order to analyze the impact, this study considers these two actors.

An analysis on the first actor: Roles of the Indian pharmaceutical industry—maintaining healthy development by changing business models

An analysis on the second actor: Roles of the Indian government, which inserted Section 3 (d) into the Patents (Amendment) Act, 2005

In conducting this study, the author divided it into the following two phases:

Phase I analyzes various indicators which demonstrate the status of the Indian pharmaceutical industry. This phase of the study analyzes the kinds of strategies pursued by the industry, taking advantage of TRIPS enforcement in 1995 and the introduction of product patents in 2005, and what kinds of outcomes were produced [1].

First, based on the work of La Croix and Kawaura, this study analyzes the business performance of the Indian pharmaceutical industry both before and after introduction of product patents. La Croix and Kawaura concluded that "when product patents are introduced into a developing country, it tends to have a negative impact on the local economy." In line with the La Croix and Kawaura approach, this study first examines the trend of stock prices. Then, it looks at sales and profit figures and the R&D investments of major pharmaceutical companies. For these analyses, this study uses comprehensive data on the Indian pharmaceutical industry compiled by the Indian government, together with the annual reports of major Indian pharmaceutical companies.

Second, this study analyzes drug development pipelines in the Indian pharmaceutical industry. Because Indian pharmaceutical companies were almost without exception applying the generic drugs business model (utilizing reverse engineering technology) until the mid-1990s or until TRIPS enforcement, there were no pipelines before the mid-1990s. This study looks into recent development pipelines of major Indian pharmaceutical companies. New drug development is conducted in a sequence of steps. The analysis tabulates the number of molecules in each development phase, from preclinical through Phase I, Phase II, and Phase III to new drug approval.

Next, this study analyzes the trend of patent applications. The Indian government drastically revised its patent law in 2005 and introduced product patents. Prior to 2005, the government set up a "mailbox" in accordance with the Patents (Amendment) Act, 1999, and it began accepting product patent applications in 1999. According to the Indian Patent Office (IPO), a total 7,945 patents had been applied for via the mailbox system as of 2005. This study utilizes comprehensive patent application data compiled by the IPO and the application records of individual Indian pharmaceutical companies.

Finally, this study analyzes trade data on pharmaceutical products. Prior to the 2005 introduction of product patents in India, many concerns were expressed by various stakeholders. For example, (a) there could be rapid entry of many patented pharmaceutical products into the Indian domestic market; (b) exports of Indian generic drugs could decline. There are basically two categories of pharmaceutical products: formulations and bulk/intermediates. This study analyzes export and import figures for both categories.

Phase II study: In order to determine if Section 3 (d) of the Patents (Amendment) Act 2005 has protected the Indian pharmaceutical industry and thereby enabled local companies to maintain healthy development, this study conducted a series of interviews with various India-based stakeholders.

3.4 Research Framework

The research framework is shown in Fig. 3.1.

Phase I of this study analyzes various data and examines how the Indian pharmaceutical industry coped with the transition of the intellectual property regime in India. Phase II, by way of a series of interviews, examines whether or not insertion of Section 3 (d) protected the Indian pharmaceutical industry against foreign-owned companies and granted local companies time to change their business models or launch new ones.

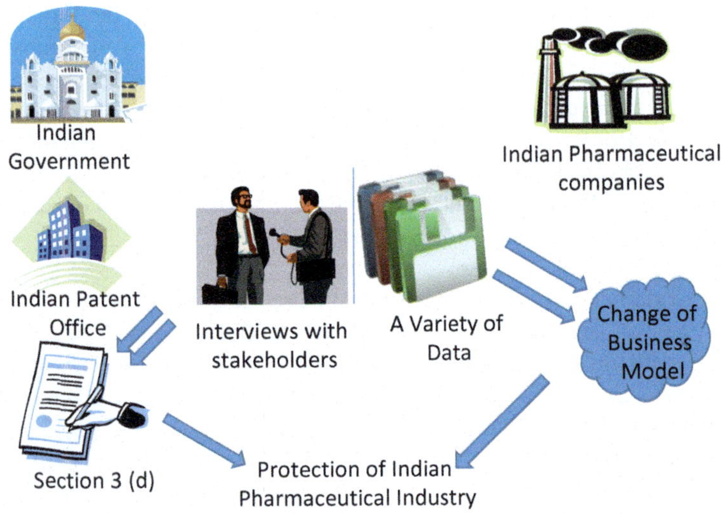

Fig. 3.1 Research framework

References

1. S. La Croix and A. Kawaura, "Product Patent Reform and Its Impact on Korea's Pharmaceutical Industry," *International Economic Journal* 10, no. 1 (1996): 109–124.

Chapter 4
Analysis of Preceding Studies

As mentioned above, TRIPS, which came into effect in 1995, basically requires all member countries to introduce product patents. Once the framework was announced, a number of researchers carried out their own studies on the impact of TRIPS on developing countries and released their research results.

Those earlier studies can be categorized into four areas: research regarding relations between developing countries and patent systems, research on the impacts of product patents, research on Section 3 (d), and research on the business model transition in the Indian pharmaceutical industry. This chapter analyzes previous research in those four areas.

4.1 Developing Countries and Patent Law

The TWN Briefing Paper, focusing on the issue of access to medicines, argues that many people die each year in developing countries due to lack of access to effective and affordable medicines [1].

The paper suggested that one of the causes of this situation was the obligation under TRIPS for governments to implement high standards for intellectual property protection, effectively eliminating competition from generic pharmaceuticals producers and eventually allowing manufacturers of branded drugs to increase the prices of their products to levels beyond the financial reach of patients in developing countries.

The paper added that many people, who feel that the current TRIPS framework tilts too heavily in favor of private rights and commercial interests and against the public interest, have expressed concerns about the legitimacy of patents on lifesaving drugs and are requesting changes or amendments to the TRIPS Agreement.

Based on a prior study which revealed that Japanese pharmaceutical industry stock prices gained 25.82% on average during a 2-month period before and after the

Y. Mitsumori, *The Indian Pharmaceutical Industry*,
SpringerBriefs in Health Care Management and Economics,
https://doi.org/10.1007/978-981-10-6790-7_4

introduction of product patents in Japan (April through May 1975), La Croix and Kawaura examined Korean pharmaceutical industry stock prices (pharmaceuticals stock price index on the Korea Stock Exchange) before and after the introduction of product patents in Korea (during the 14-month period November 1985–December 1986) and found that they had dropped 74% over that period [2].

Recognizing that the impact of product patents on an industry tends to be affected by such factors as (a) the initial state of R&D activity, (b) industry structure, and (c) industrial behavior patterns, they concluded from their analysis that a country which is close to developed country status, such as Singapore, may experience welfare gains as a result of adopting more stringent IPR laws, whereas a country in the early stages of development, such as Indonesia, is likely to experience welfare losses #18 in the wake of strengthening of such laws.

Based on their own study of the Korean experience, they concluded that transition to stronger IPR laws in developing countries may generate economic losses for those countries.

Yun Sun Hee (尹宣熙), in his presentation at a joint event organized by the University of Tokyo and Kyoto University in 2009, closely examined the 1986 revisions to the Korean Patents Act [3].

"In the 1980s, advanced countries which were facing fierce competition in all fields but especially in the area of IT, strengthened their IPR protection in order to accelerate state-of-the-art technology development. The US government, which regarded inadequate IPR protection as a significant barrier to fair trade, required all of its trading partners to strengthen their IPR laws."

As a result, the Korean government was coming under increasing pressure from the US government to introduce a stronger IPR system, according to Prof. Yun.

The US regarded IPR protection in Korea as inadequate and requested the Korean government to introduce full-scale IPR protection, threatening imposition of Section 301 of the Trade Act. The US government and the Korean Government engaged in a series of negotiations over the issue and ultimately the Korean government agreed to strengthen its patent law and introduce product patents into the law, Prof. Yun explained.

He added: "The bill for revision of the patent law went through the Korean National Assembly on December 18, 1986 and the revised patent law was promulgated on December 31. The new patent law came into force on July 1, 1987."

As La Croix and Kawaura found, after Korea introduced the product patent in its patent law, pharmaceutical industry stock prices fell by 74%, on average.

There are several studies on the impact caused by the introduction of product patents into Japanese patent law. Hiroshi Akimoto, in his presentation titled, "R&D Strategy of the Japanese Pharmaceutical Industry and Bio Technology," (at Roppongi Hills) said: "In Japan, product patents were introduced in 1976. From that time, R&D activity in the Japanese pharmaceutical industry accelerated, leading to an increase in the number of new drugs developed in Japan" [4].

P. G. Sampath analyzed the impact of product patents on developing countries after the TRIPS Agreement imposed a requirement for stronger intellectual property protection on all member countries, including developing countries. Sampath argued that product patent protection in India is a very decisive factor in determining access to medicines, not only in India but also in other developing countries, and that losses in the Indian industry following India's move to full-scale TRIPS compliance have been very high [5].

He added that this meant that the Indian pharmaceutical industry would have to focus on how to survive in the newly competitive market rather than on public access to medicines. Sampath classified Indian pharmaceutical companies into three groups by revenue and analyzed the respective strategies of each group.

Group 1 comprises large pharmaceutical companies with annual sales revenue of 300 crore rupees or more (Group 1). Group 1 pharmaceutical companies have been developing NCEs and value-added generic drugs and marketing them not only in India but also in regulated markets. These firms have accumulated high profits from sales of generic products in regulated markets, and they plow much of that profit into R&D. It seems to take longer for them to launch the next new blockbuster #19 NCEs in India; however, these companies have been gearing up research on NCEs, and value-added generics such as drug delivery systems (DDS) #20, and biopharmaceuticals.

Group 2 consists of medium-scale pharmaceutical companies with annual sales revenue of between 100 and 300 crore rupees (Group 2). Since Group 2 pharmaceutical companies have little or no capability to invest in R&D, these manufacturers focus on production of simple generic drugs (vanilla generics). They will attempt to establish themselves as niche players in contract research and manufacturing.

Group 3 comprises small-scale pharmaceutical companies with annual sales revenue of less than 100 crore (Group 3). Following enactment of Schedule M of the Drugs and Cosmetics Act on minimum Good Manufacturing Practice (GMP) #21 (GMP standards), it is thought that this segment will undergo major consolidation over the coming 10 years. Group 3 pharmaceutical companies, which can upgrade their plants to meet the GMP standards as stipulated in Schedule M of the Drugs and Cosmetics Act, seek to benefit from contract manufacturing. Since the standards stipulated in Schedule M are much lower than the WHO standards for GMPs, these small pharmaceutical companies appear to concentrate on carrying out contract manufacturing for Group 2 companies in India which are looking at satisfying the demand for generics in unregulated and semi-regulated markets or directly supplying foreign partners in such markets.

4.2 Impact of Introduction of Product Patents

Joseph, R. K., analyzed the impacts of introduction of product patents into trade in Indian pharmaceutical products [6].

Joseph pointed out that, when it was decided to introduce product patents in India, a number of concerns were expressed, including the following: (a) the Indian pharmaceutical industry would sustain a negative impact, (b) Indian generic companies would not be able to copy drugs patented outside of India by reverse engineering them and would be prevented from marketing them both in India and overseas, (c) Indian exports of pharmaceutical products would decline, (d) the balance of trade would worsen, and (e) imports of formulations would increase.

Utilizing actual trade data for the period between 1990–1991 and 2007–2008, Joseph analyzed the trends of the pharmaceutical trade in India in order to clarify what happened before and after introduction of product patents.

He found that (a) exports of pharmaceutical products increased rapidly; (b) categories of export products changed from intermediates and bulk substances to formulations; (c) prior to introduction of product patents, some concerns had been raised about the likelihood of a rapid increase in imports of foreign pharmaceuticals after product patents were introduced in India; however, the trade data showed that imports of foreign products did not rapidly expand; and (d) imports of intermediates and bulk substances rose steeply.

From the data, he found that Indian pharmaceutical companies were importing intermediates and bulk substances, producing formulations (finished products) using these materials, and exporting those formulations to other countries.

Imports of formulations did not grow to any great extent. Joseph argued that the reason for this was that the number of patents granted in India to that point had been restricted due to the limited patentability provisions of the current Indian Patent Law.

Chadha analyzed the impact of stronger patent legislation on patenting activity in Indian pharmaceutical companies. Chadha used data from 321 pharmaceutical companies on the Prowess Database of the Centre for Monitoring Indian Economy (CMIE). Companies which invest more than 1% of their revenues into R&D areas are required to report the amount of such expenditure to the Prowess database [7].

As a result of analyses utilizing methods such as the Poisson regression model and the Zero-inflated model, Chadha found that the stricter patent regime has stimulated patenting activity in the Indian pharmaceutical industry.

Chadha noted that, because the Indian industry is more active in R&D and patenting compared to pharmaceutical industries in other developing countries, welfare losses arising from the higher prices generated by a more stringent patent regime would be lower in India compared to the other developing countries because Indian drug manufacturers can use their ownership of patents to penetrate export markets.

From the data analysis, Chadha found that there were gestation lags of around 2 years between R&D activities and patent applications in India and that patenting tended to occur at a later stage of the R&D sequence in developing countries such as India.

Chaudhuri et al. first examined whether introduction of product patents pushed up prices of drugs in India and then, focusing on a family of antibacterial agents called quinolones #22, predicted the extent to which quinolone prices could increase after product patents were introduced in India [8].

Quinolones are the latest-generation molecules available in India. Chaudhuri et al. selected them because they are drugs of choice for treatment of a large number of bacterial infections, and several molecules within the quinolone subsegment were still under US patent protection during the sampling period. Using detailed product level data on monthly pharmaceutical prices and sales over the 2-year period January 1999-December 2000, Chaudhuri et al. estimated key price, expenditure elasticities, and supply-side parameters for quinolones in the Indian pharmaceutical market.

The researchers assumed that, if product patents were introduced in India, all domestic products whose active pharmaceutical ingredients were protected by patents would be eliminated from the Indian market. They calculated the impact of product patents introduction based on the assumption that all domestically produced quinolones would be eliminated from the Indian market. Based on their own analysis, Chaudhuri et al. concluded that concerns about the potentially adverse welfare effects of TRIPS in developing countries might have some basis.

They also calculated potential welfare losses incurred by the introduction of product patents in India both with and without price controls. It was estimated that welfare losses of between US$144 million and US$450 million (in the quinolone subsegment area) would likely be sustained by the Indian economy as a result of introduction of product patents. On the other hand, foreign-owned companies could enjoy a profit gain of US$53 million without price controls or US$19.6 million with price controls. Based on these figures, Chaudhuri et al. argued that these figures were "just a small fraction of the annual sales of big pharmaceutical firms in this sub-segment."

They also pointed out that, if IPR were to be enforced without price controls, this would boost the incentives for foreign-owned companies to market their products in developing countries and use licensing more extensively; however, that would be accompanied by substantial price increases for patented products. Conversely, if IPR were to be enforced with price controls, this would prevent patent holders from exploiting their market power; however, it would diminish the incentive for such firms to sell their products in developing countries. The researchers concluded that it would be quite difficult to design a combination policy which totally neutralized the adverse effects of TRIPS compliance on consumer welfare.

Grace analyzed the impact of revision of patent systems on the Indian and Chinese pharmaceutical industries, based on academic papers, press articles, and the reports of stock market analysts [9].

He explained that he had chosen this issue because India and China are important suppliers of low-priced active pharmaceutical ingredients and finished products, both domestically and to developing countries, and there had been much concern expressed about the potential for introduction of product patents to destroy those industries and possibly generate higher prices for medicines.

Grace noted that, because introduction of product patents in India meant that Indian firms would have reduced revenue options for domestic sales of pharmaceutical products due to generic copies of newer drugs having become illegal, Indian firms have shifted to exporting to the more profitable regulated markets in order to compensate for that revenue loss.

He also pointed out that large Indian pharmaceutical companies (such as Ranbaxy and Dr. Reddy's) have increased their R&D investments and launched development of NCEs and novel drug delivery systems. However, Grace also noted that Indian pharmaceutical companies are targeting treatments for diseases that are prevalent in more affluent countries, such as cardiovascular products, despite there being a clear need for greater investment in development of treatments for neglected diseases.

Based on published sources and a series of personal interviews, Lanjouw analyzed the theoretical implications for India of introducing product patents for pharmaceuticals [10].

Conclusion of the TRIPS Agreement with its requirement for all members, including developing countries, to introduce product patents, raised concerns that such an introduction would push up drug prices in developing countries and, as a result, the general public would lose access to medicines. However, multinational enterprises (MNEs) countered such opinions by claiming that patent regimes would bring benefits in the form of focusing more research on tropical diseases and encouraging greater domestic and foreign investment in local research activities.

Lanjouw analyzed the impact of introduction of product patents into the Indian pharmaceuticals field based on this debate.

From his own research, Lanjouw concluded that the Indian pharmaceutical industry would continue to enjoy competitive advantages over foreign-owned companies, even after 2005, because India's low manufacturing costs would continue to give local companies an edge in the Indian domestic market, despite their potential loss of first-mover advantage through introduction of product patents.

On the other hand, Lanjouw pointed out that two factors which currently help to push down drug prices in the Indian market—the low average income of India's general public and the lack of a medical insurance scheme—are likely to begin to change over the next decade and, as a result, continuing low prices cannot be assured. Regarding pricing by MNEs, Lanjouw argued that, while MNEs might seek to maximize profits in the world market, they might not be setting prices to maximize profits in the Indian market because the politics of drug price regulation could dictate price ceilings.

Lanjouw concluded that, as already noted, large Indian pharmaceutical companies are increasing their R&D expenditure as a percentage of sales and are beginning to move in the direction of new molecule discovery and value-added generics and that the effect of Indian product patents introduction was not to encourage this process but rather to put an end to imitation.

4.3 Section 3 (d) of Indian Patents (Amendment) Act, 2005

Basheer, S., and Reddy, T. P., examined Section 3 (d), a controversial section inserted into the Patents (Amendment) Act, 2005, utilizing the case of Novartis' "Gleevec," and presented their own alternative section [11].

They first pointed out that Section 3 (d) was inserted into the Patent (Amendment) Act, 2005 to prevent "evergreening" #23 by denying a known chemical molecule form patentability unless it shows enhanced efficacy.

Basheer and Reddy stated: "Section 3 (d) aims to prevent 'evergreening' by prohibiting the patenting of new forms of existing pharmaceutical substances that do not demonstrate significantly enhanced 'efficacy'."

They went on to argue that the Madras High Court's ruling on the Novartis case was correct. On the other hand, they argued that Section 3 (d) contains several "flaws" and some vague words/phrases such as "efficacy" and "significant enhancement." They suggested that this was due to the section having been drafted in a "slipshod" manner.

Regarding the word "efficacy," they argued that, if "efficacy" is defined as "therapeutic efficacy," some technology such as DDS, one of the strengths of the Indian pharmaceutical industry, is exempted from patent protection.

Basheer and Reddy also argued that Section 3 (d) is a unique clause which can only be found in the Indian patent law and that no other country determines patentability of a molecule based on efficacy. They added that it is not the Patent Office but rather the Department of Health (or equivalent healthcare regulatory agency) that is responsible for determining whether or not a molecule is efficacious.

They also noted that there are some discrepancies between the main body of Section 3 (d) and the Explanation: The main body of Section 3 (d) states "enhancement of known efficacy," whereas the Explanation uses broader terminology: "significant difference in properties with regard to efficacy." They argue that this discrepancy could lead to different results when patentability of the new use of a new form of a known substance is assessed.

Based on the above discussion, Basheer and Reddy presented their own alternative wording for Section 3 (d), as follows:

What are not inventions: The following are not inventions within the meaning of this Act ...

(d) A new form of a known substance, unless it differs significantly in properties with regard to efficacy, when compared with the known substance, or the mere discovery of any new property or new use for a known substance or of the mere use of a known process, machine or apparatus unless such process results in a new product or employs at least one new reactant.

Explanation: For the purposes of this clause, salts, esters, ethers, polymorphs, metabolites, pure form, particle size, isomers, mixtures of isomers, complexes, combinations and other structurally similar forms of a known substance shall be deemed to constitute "new forms of a known substance."

For the purposes of this clause, a "known substance," against which the efficacy of a "new form" ought to be compared, shall be taken to be a substance which is not "new," in that it does satisfy the "novelty" criterion for patentability.

For the purposes of establishing that a "new form" differs significantly in properties with regard to efficacy, an applicant must provide data comparing the efficacy of the new form with that of a "known" substance. Such data need not prove this "difference" in property as a matter of statistical certainty, nor does the applicant have to provide actual evidence of trials in humans. Instead, the applicant has to demonstrate a reasonable correlation between the efficacy claimed and the data provided in support of this. Such reasonable evidence of the correlation can be established by relying on, inter alia, statistically relevant data documenting the activity of the new form and/or known substance, documentary evidence, data generated using in vitro assays, or from testing in an animal model, other preclinical test data or any combination thereof.

For the purposes of this clause, a determination as to whether a difference in property with regard to "efficacy" is "significant," shall be assessed with reference to the views of a person skilled in the relevant art.

The version proposed by Basheer and Reddy clarified the following four points:

(a) Avoided using the word "derivatives" by replacing it with "other structurally similar forms of a known substance" in order to clarify the meaning.
(b) Defined "known substance."
(c) In order to establish that a "new form" differs significantly in properties with regard to efficacy, a patent applicant must provide data comparing the efficacy of the new form with that of a "known" substance. However, the applicant does not need to prove the "difference" statistically or to submit human trial data; instead, the applicant has to demonstrate a reasonable correlation using in vitro assay or animal test data.
(d) Determination as to whether a difference in property with regard to "efficacy" is "significant," to be assessed with reference to the opinion of a specialist.

4.4 Transition of Indian Pharmaceutical Industry Business Model

Chaturvedi and Chataway conducted a documentary study based on prior literature, corporate annual reports, and two-phase face-to-face interviews, in order to determine how Indian pharmaceutical companies have changed their business model from a reverse engineering one to that of technologically advanced and sophisticated organizations capable of catering to a variety of markets in the face of a drastic change in intellectual property rights frameworks [12].

According to Chaturvedi and Chataway, as Indian pharmaceutical companies changed their business models, they rapidly increased investment in R&D: Whereas the Indian pharmaceutical industry's R&D investment was a mere Rs. 3 crores in FY1965, it rapidly grew to Rs. 140 crores by FY1995 and to Rs. 200 crores by FY2002. According to IDMA, R&D expenditure is expected to reach Rs. 1000 crores by FY2004. And, along with the increase in R&D investment came a steep rise in the number of ANDA and DMF filings. The researchers reported that Indian pharmaceutical companies filed a total 392 ANDAs in 2002 and 112 ANDAs in 2003, bringing the Indian share of total ANDAs to 23% in 2003. In parallel, Indian pharmaceutical companies filed a large number of DMF applications: 126 DMFs in 2003, bringing the Indian share of DMF filings to 30%.

Chaturvedi and Chataway, through face-to-face interviews with each of the major Indian companies, found that their strategies to cope with the new patent regime differ from one company to another. For instance, Ranbaxy focuses on development of Novel Drug Delivery Systems (NDDS) rather than NCE discovery in order to avoid the risks associated with discovery and development of NCEs. Dr. Reddy's is placing emphasis on NCE discovery but also gearing for NDDS and generics development. Cipla, Nicholas Piramal India Limited (NPIL), and Sun Pharmaceutical are intensifying their research and market activities but on new, improved, and value-added products rather than on new drugs. Meanwhile, other companies, including Lupin, have been taking a combination of traditional strategies with research activities.

Kale et al., through two-phase interviews with various Indian pharmaceutical industry stakeholders, showed that Indian pharmaceutical companies have evolved from a reverse engineering model to that of a complex, knowledge-based industry with advanced technology and NCE development capability [13].

Using a "capability creation model," they showed how the Indian pharmaceutical industry has developed from the "duplicative imitation stage" (companies devoted to reverse engineering) through the "creative imitation stage" (companies engaged in generics R&D activities) and the "intermediate capability stage" (companies engaged in analog and NDDS research) to, finally, the "mature capability stage" (companies initiating original NCE research).

Kale et al. argued that the change of IP framework due to TRIPS forced Indian pharmaceutical companies to change their business model from a conventional reverse engineering or imitation one to an innovative R&D model. They also pointed out Indian pharmaceutical companies have been transforming from a conventional duplicative imitation model to a mature capability model by fully utilizing the fundamental knowledge that the manufacturers had accumulated in the course of their reverse engineering practices.

4.5 Working Hypothesis

The analyses in Sect. 4.4 show that the Indian pharmaceutical industry has changed from a purely generic drugs business model based on reverse engineering to an integrated business model dealing with both generic and brand-name drugs, taking advantage of TRIPS enforcement in 1995 and introduction of product patents in 2005. These analyses suggest that the Indian pharmaceutical industry's self-efforts served to mitigate the negative impact of introduction of product patents, as shown in several prior studies.

Based on this observation, a "working hypothesis" is set up here in order to operationalize the hypothesis set up in Chap. 3.

The working hypothesis is as follows:

Indian government effort—inserting the safeguarding clause Section 3 (d) into the Patents (Amendment) Act, 2005—and the Indian pharmaceutical industry's self-help efforts—changing its business model from a conventional purely generics business model to an integrated business model; embracing both generic drugs (off-patent drugs) and brand-name drugs (patented drugs)—created a synergistic effect which eventually mitigated the negative impact that a developing country would normally sustain in the wake of introduction of product patents.

If this working hypothesis is proved, this study will consider that its main hypothesis—that insertion of Section 3 (d) into the Patents (Amendment) Act, 2005 by the Indian government positively influenced the Indian pharmaceutical industry's development after 2005, avoiding the negative impact of introduction of product patents—is proved. Many developing countries and international NGOs/NPOs, which provide support to those countries, expressed concerns when the TRIPS Agreement in 1995 required all member countries to introduce strict patent protection, including product patents.

On the other hand, developed countries and MNEs (multinational enterprises) expressed support for introduction of a strict patent system in India. This issue caused major conflict, not just in India but worldwide. This study analyzed the relevant literature, reports, and commissioned papers across four categories: (a) developing countries and patent law; (b) impact of introduction of product patents; (c) Section 3 (d) of the Patents (Amendment) Act, 2005; (d) transition of business model of Indian pharmaceutical industry.

Most of the source materials were written prior to 2005, and some others written after 2005 used pre-2005 data. If there are some discrepancies between the conclusions of some of those prior studies and that of this study's conclusion, they may be attributable to the time difference.

References

1. "TRIPS, Patents and Access to Medicines: Proposals for Clarification and Reform" (briefing paper, Third World Network, June 2001).
2. S. La Croix and A. Kawaura, "Product Patent Reform and Its Impact on Korea's Pharmaceutical Industry," *International Economic Journal* 10, no. 1 (1996): 109–124.
3. Yun Sun Hee, "Korean Patent System for Innovation" (presentation, meeting of the National Innovation System, Competition and Cooperation – The Patent System in Next Generation – by the University of Tokyo and Kyoto University, Kyoto University, June 11, 2009): 5.
4. Hiroshi Akimoto, "R&D Strategy of the Japanese Pharmaceutical Industry and Bio Technology" (presentation material, Path of Bio Innovation and Future Development, Industry-Academy-Govt. Collaboration Workshop, Roppongi Hills, March 10, 2009): 5.
5. Padmashree Sampath, "Economic Aspects of Access to Medicines after 2005: Product Patent Protection and Emerging Firm Strategies in the Indian Pharmaceutical Industry," *United Nations University-Institute for New Technologies [UNU-INTECH]* (Jan. 2005).
6. R. Joseph, "India's Trade in Drugs and Pharmaceuticals: Emerging Trends, Opportunities and Challenges" (RIS discussion paper, no. 159, Nov. 2009): 1–45.
7. Alka Chadha, "Trips and Patenting Activity: Evidence from the Indian Pharmaceutical Industry" (working paper, no. 0512, National University of Singapore, Department of Economics, 2005.

8. Shubham Chaudhuri et al., "Estimating the Effects of Global Patent Protection in Pharmaceuticals: A Case Study of Quinolones in India" (NBER working paper, no. 10159, Dec. 2003, revised in 2006).
9. Cheri Grace, "The Effect of Changing Intellectual Property on Pharmaceutical Industry Prospects in India and China: Considerations for Access to Medicines," *DFID Health Systems Resource Centre* (June 2004).
10. Jean Lanjouw, "The Introduction of Pharmaceutical Product Patents in India: 'Heartless Exploitation of the Poor and Suffering'?" (NBER working paper, no. 6366, Jan. 1998).
11. Shamnad Basheer and T. Reddy, "The 'Efficacy' of Indian Patent Law: Ironing out the Creases in Section 3 (d)," *scripted* 5, no. 2 (August 2008).
12. Kalpana Chaturvedi and Joanna Chataway, "Strategic Integration of Knowledge in Indian Pharmaceutical Firms: Creating Competencies for Innovation," *International Journal of Business Innovation and Research* 1, no. 1/2 (2006): 27–50.
13. Dinar Kale et al., "Reconfiguration of Competencies for Innovation – The Case of the Indian Pharmaceutical Industry" (presentation at a conference in honor of Keith Pavitt, Open University Business School, Nov. 13–15, 2003).

Chapter 5
Analysis of Indian Pharmaceutical Industry Indicators: Data Analysis

Following the framework shown in Chap. 3, this chapter conducts a first-step analysis—analyzing several indicators which reflect the Indian pharmaceutical industry's business activities. This chapter looks at the kinds of strategies adopted by Indian pharmaceutical companies, taking advantage of enforcement of the TRIPS Agreement and introduction of product patents in 2005, and also analyzes the resulting outcomes of their decisions.

5.1 Data Analysis Methodology

Prior studies described in Chap. 4 show that introduction of a stringent patent framework can adversely affect a developing country's economy.

La Croix and Kawaura noted that when a stricter patent framework is introduced in a developing country, it tends to cause economic losses [1]. If their conclusion is correct, a developing country may sustain economic losses when product patents are introduced.

For this study, using a variety of data, it was decided to compare the performance of the Indian pharmaceutical industry before and after 2005, the year in which product patents were introduced in India. Six indicators were analyzed: stock prices, business performance (sales and profits), R&D investments, new drug development pipelines, patent applications, and trade activities.

First, this study analyzed stock prices of Indian pharmaceutical companies. In order to clarify whether or not La Croix's and Kawaura's conclusion can be applied to India, this study compared Indian pharmaceutical companies' stock prices before and after the introduction of product patents in 2005.

Y. Mitsumori, *The Indian Pharmaceutical Industry*,
SpringerBriefs in Health Care Management and Economics,
https://doi.org/10.1007/978-981-10-6790-7_5

Almost all large Indian pharmaceutical companies are listed on stock exchanges.

Using a search engine on the Indian National Stock Exchange website, this study extracted stock prices of large Indian pharmaceutical companies before and after product patents were introduced and drew a graph.

However, stock prices are just one among several indicators that reflect economic and business activities. Accordingly, this study decided to analyze several other indicators which more directly reflect business activities.

For the second analysis, this study decided to analyze the business performance figures for leading pharmaceutical companies in India. Out of a range of indicators, it was decided to use sales and profit figures which directly reflect each company's business performance.

Through this series of studies, the author learned that several large Indian companies had modified their business models and launched new drug discovery and development programs. That is why this study also examined R&D activities as a third-step analysis. The author collected R&D investment figures and extracted supporting information, such as reporting of construction of a new R&D center, from company annual reports and other materials in order to analyze the R&D strategies/tactics of each company.

The third-step analysis suggested that some Indian companies have been strengthening their development pipelines.

As a fourth-step analysis, this study looked at development pipelines. Development pipelines directly show the outcomes of each company's new drug discovery/development effort. This study analyzed the progress of each company's new drug discovery/development effort.

From the third-step and fourth-step analyses, it would appear that some companies could be seeking intellectual property rights protection. As a fifth-step analysis, the author decided to analyze patent application numbers. Utilizing the Indian Patent Office (IPO) website, this study collected data on patent applications in the pharmaceuticals field. In addition, utilizing a search engine on the IPO website, patent applications data for each major pharmaceutical company were extracted [2].

And, last but not least, this study analyzed trade data as a sixth-step analysis. Prior to the introduction of product patents in India, a number of concerns were expressed, for example, entry into the Indian market by foreign-owned companies, domination of the local market by imported goods and products, and a consequent loss of market presence for Indian pharmaceutical companies.

To examine the balance between local pharmaceutical manufacturers and foreign-owned companies in the Indian market, this study analyzed data on exports from and imports into India. Indian pharmaceutical firms are exporting/importing bulk/intermediates and formulations. This study collected trade data on both bulk/intermediates and formulations before and after 2005.

Through a series of data analyses, this study sought to determine if introduction of product patents in India, a developing country, had a negative impact on the Indian pharmaceutical industry, as was suggested by a prior study.

Unlike the situation in advanced countries, data in India tend to be incomplete. Sometimes, data items with different bases are mixed together.

In this study, the author made best efforts to gather integrated and comprehensive data. In order to compensate for possible inconsistencies in the data, this study conducted on-site interviews. Analyses based on those on-site interviews appear in Chap. 6. In Chap. 6, (a) relations between financial/business performance data and the Patents (Amendment) Act, 2005 and (b) relations between financial/business data and Section 3 (d) are analyzed.

5.2 Indian Pharmaceutical Companies Stock Price Analysis

La Croix and Kawaura analyzed pharmaceutical industry stock prices in Japan and Korea before and after introduction of product patents in each country. They concluded that when stronger patents, such as product patents, are introduced in an advanced country (or nearly advanced country), introduction of such patents tends to produce welfare gains; however, when product patents are introduced in a developing country, the effect is likely to be welfare loss [1].

India is categorized as a developing country. In order to test if the conclusion drawn by La Croix and Kawaura could apply to India, this study analyzed stock prices of Indian pharmaceutical companies before and after introduction of product patents in India.

If their conclusion is correct, stock prices in India, a developing country, should have fallen in the wake of introduction of product patents in 2005.

For this study, the author decided to analyze National Stock Exchange (NSE) prices. There are 23 stock markets in India. The two largest markets are the NSE and the Bombay Stock Exchange (BSE). Several major Indian pharmaceutical companies are listed on the NSE, which was established in 1994 [3].

The analysis found that the stock prices of the four leading pharmaceutical companies in India had shown an upward trend since April 4, 2005, when the Patents (Amendment) Act, 2005 was enacted.

It was decided to focus on companies that had changed their business model from the conventional "exclusively generic model" to an "integrated business model" which deals with both generic drugs (off-patent drugs) and brand-name drugs (patented drugs). Accordingly, this study initially considered five top Indian companies—Ranbaxy, Dr. Reddy's, Lupin, Sun Pharmaceutical and Cipla—to test the hypothesis that government action, in the form of insertion of Section 3 (d), and self-efforts by certain members of the industry (change of business model) created a synergistic effect. Because only large pharmaceutical companies could adopt the

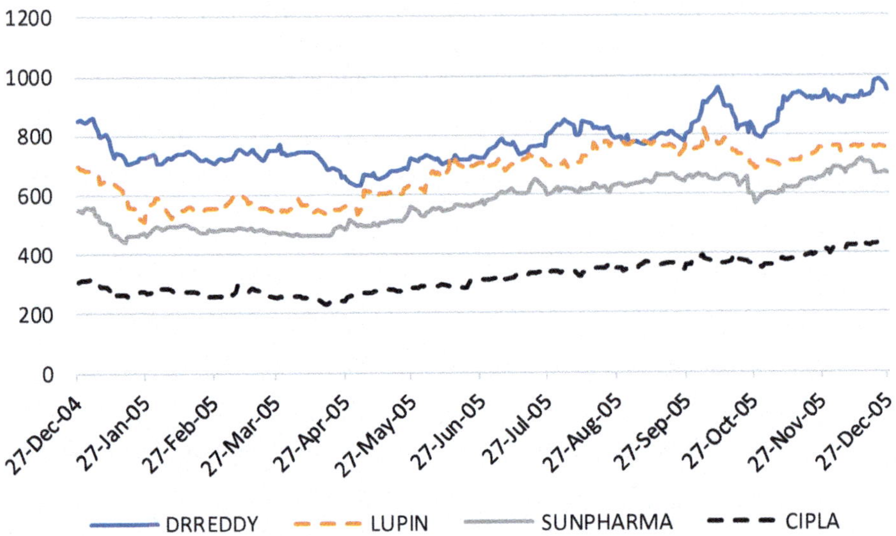

Fig. 5.1 Stock prices of Indian major pharmaceutical companies (*Source*: The National Stock Exchange (NSE), Ref. [3])

integrated business model and smaller companies could not change their business models, large companies had to be targets of this study.

Since Ranbaxy was purchased by Daiichi-Sankyo in 2008 and later acquired by Sun Pharmaceutical in 2015, the company was dropped from this study. Ultimately, four major companies were selected: Dr. Reddy's, Lupin, Sun Pharma, and Cipla.

Figure 5.1 shows stock prices of four Indian pharmaceutical companies—Dr. Reddy's, Lupin, Sun Pharma, Cipla—on the National Stock Exchange. Closing prices between December 27, 2004 and December 27, 2005 were plotted.

The Patents (Amendment) Act, 2005 was enacted on April 4, 2005, and came into force, retroactively, on January 1, 2005 in India. In the La Croix and Kawaura study, the researchers plotted stock prices during a 2-month period from before to after the introduction of product patents in Japan (during the 2-month period of April–May 1975) and pharmaceuticals stock price index on the Korea Stock Exchange before and after the introduction of product patents in Korea (during the 14-month period of November 1985–December 1986) [1].

In the case of India, a presidential order was issued on December 26, 2004, the revision bill for the Act passed through Parliament, and the Act was revised on April 4, 2005. Taking that process into consideration, this study decided to plot stock prices between December 27, 2004 and December 27, 2005. Stock prices tend to fluctuate due to a variety of factors. However, it can be said that the stock prices of all four companies showed an upward trend during the period.

Table 5.1 Production of Indian pharmaceutical industry

	1950–1951	1960–1961	1970–1971	1980–1981	1990–1991	2000–2001
Manufacturers (No.)	200		2,300	6,400	16,000	20,000
Investment (Rs. Mil)	50	560	2,250	6,000	9,500	30,000
R&D Expenditure (Rs. Mil)			100	290	800	4,000
Production (Rs. Mil)	100	1,130	4,000	14,400	45,700	228,870
Exports (Rs. Mil)		16	85	463	7,848	87,290
Imports (Rs. Mil)		176	243	968	4,075	29,800

Source: H. Bhojwani, Ref. [4]

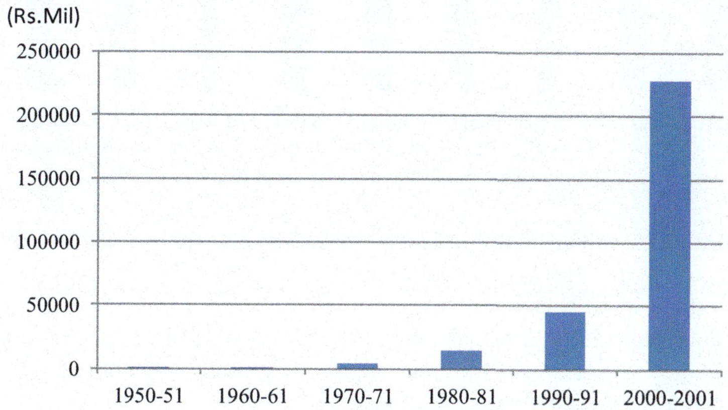

Fig. 5.2 Production trends in the Indian pharmaceutical industry (*Source*: H. Bhojwani, Ref. [4])

5.3 Business Performance Analysis of Indian Pharmaceutical Companies: Trend of Sales and Profits

As mentioned above, the Patents Act, 1970 had a significant impact on the pharmaceutical industry in India. The Patents Act, 1970 only provided protection for process patents #24. Under that Act, Indian drug companies could copy pharmaceutical products that were otherwise patented in foreign countries, which led to a boom in production of generic drugs in India.

Table 5.1 shows the production trends in the Indian pharmaceutical industry between 1950 and 2000. In India, production of pharmaceutical products, the number of pharmaceutical companies, and trade (exports and imports) expanded rapidly from the 1970s. This growth is attributed to enactment of the Patents Act, 1970 [4].

Figure 5.2 was drawn from Table 5.1. Immediately after India gained its independence from Britain in 1947, there was almost no pharmaceutical industry in India. As mentioned earlier, pharmaceutical production began to grow rapidly from the 1970s [4].

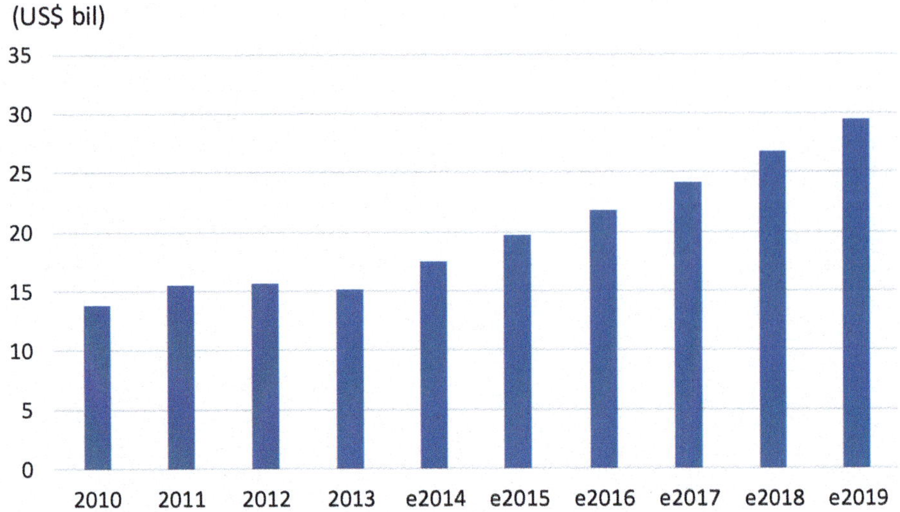

Fig. 5.3 Indian pharmaceutical market 2010–2019 (*Source*: METI, Ref. [6])

According to "Indian Pharmaceutical Market Outlook 2009–2024" by Visiongain, pharmaceutical production in India increased from US$3 billion in 1997 to US$9.7 billion in 2008 and to US$10.7 billion in 2009. The annual growth rate was 15% in 2008 and 11% in 2009, showing that the Indian pharmaceutical industry not only managed to cope with the introduction of product patents in 2005 but also maintained a strong growth rate since then [5].

Figure 5.3 shows the Indian pharmaceutical market between 2010 and 2019 (estimated figures between 2014 and 2019). The report estimated Indian pharmaceutical market would grow at an annual growth rate of 10.8% after 2014 and would reach US$ 29.5 billion in 2019 [6].

Next, in order to analyze business performance before and after introduction of product patents in India, this study analyzed the sales and profit figures for four leading Indian companies: Dr. Reddy's (Fig. 5.4), Lupin (Fig. 5.5), Sun (Fig. 5.6), and Cipla (Fig. 5.7) [7–10].

The four figures below (Figs. 5.4, 5.5, 5.6, and 5.7) show that these four Indian pharmaceutical companies successfully expanded their sales revenues, even after 2005, the year in which product patents were introduced in India. During the period, all four companies actively engaged in M&A, which helped to drive sales revenue growth.

Profits tend to fluctuate due to a variety of factors, including business climate, regulations, foreign exchange rates, and company strategies. However, all four companies showed upward trends during the period. Dr. Reddy's recorded a loss in 2009 due to the sluggish business performance of its Betapharm subsidiary.

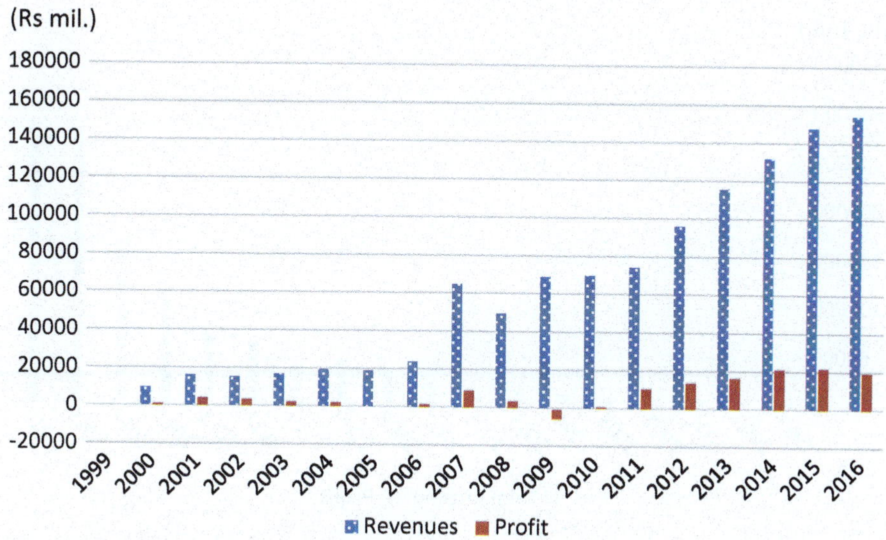

Fig. 5.4 Dr. Reddy's revenues and profit (2000–2016) (*Source*: Dr. Reddy's, Ref. [7])

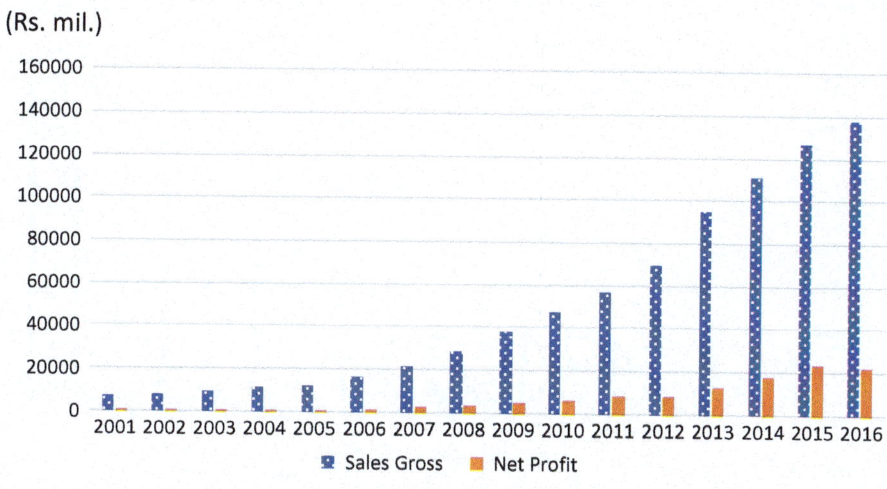

Fig. 5.5 Lupin's sales gross and profit (2001–2016) (*Source*: Lupin, Ref. [8])

Fig. 5.6 Sun's total income and profit (1999–2016) (*Source*: Sun Pharma, Ref. [9])

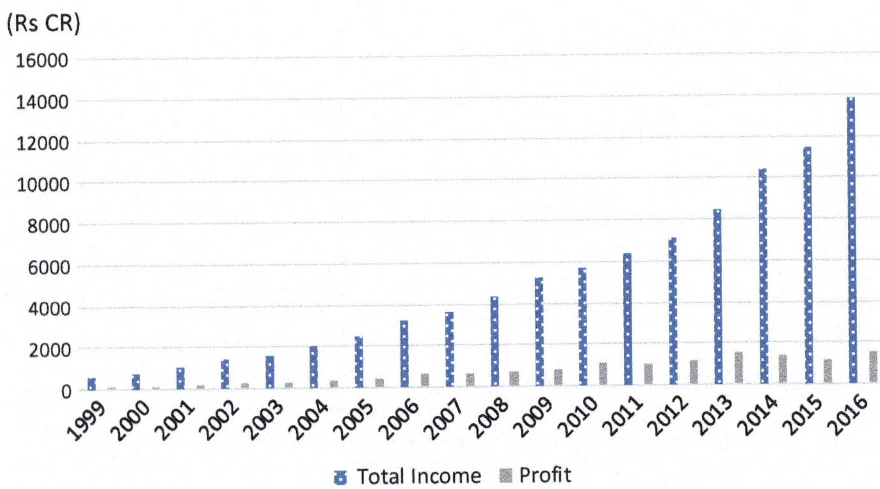

Fig. 5.7 Cipla's total income and profit (1999–2016) (*Source*: Cipla, Ref. [10])

These graphs show that all four Indian pharmaceutical companies succeeded in achieving healthy growth, even after introduction of product patents in India in 2005.

5.4 Trend of R&D Investment in Indian Pharmaceutical Industry

Next, this study analyzed R&D investment by Indian pharmaceutical companies.

As noted earlier, under the Patents Act, 1970, Indian pharmaceutical companies were "legally" able to reverse engineer patented drugs, and they produced and sold these "mimic products" as "generic drugs," not only within India but also in other countries. Due to the reverse engineering business model, the Indian pharmaceutical industry enjoyed rapid sales expansion.

Because, at that time, all Indian pharmaceutical companies were exclusively producing and selling "generic drugs," they made minimal investment in R&D.

However, as prior studies have demonstrated, some major Indian pharmaceutical companies began increasing R&D investment and launching value-added generic drugs such as DDS as well as NCEs, taking advantage of the TRIPS Agreement and introduction of product patents.

There is a very large difference between the amount of investment required for simple generic drug development and the amounts required for development of value-added generic drugs or NCEs.

Figure 5.8 shows R&D investments by Indian pharmaceutical firms between 1991 and 2006. As mentioned above, Indian companies exclusively produced and sold simple generic drugs up until the 1990s. However, some major companies began developing value-added generic drugs and NCEs around the mid-1990s, taking advantage of the TRIPS Agreement and introduction of product patents in 2005. Reflecting the trend, R&D investments began to increase in the mid-1990s and rose sharply in the 2000s [11, 12].

Figure 5.8 shows that, in 1991, total R&D investment by the Indian pharmaceutical industry was a mere US$36.5 million. Over the ensuing decade, it doubled to reach US$73.6 million by 2000. Thereafter, it rose sharply to hit US$495.2 million by 2006.

In fact, the R&D investment trend differs somewhat from company to company, depending on each company's R&D strategy. Some companies decided to pour large amounts of money into launching NCE development or value-added generic drug development; some others may have elected to hold R&D investment at almost

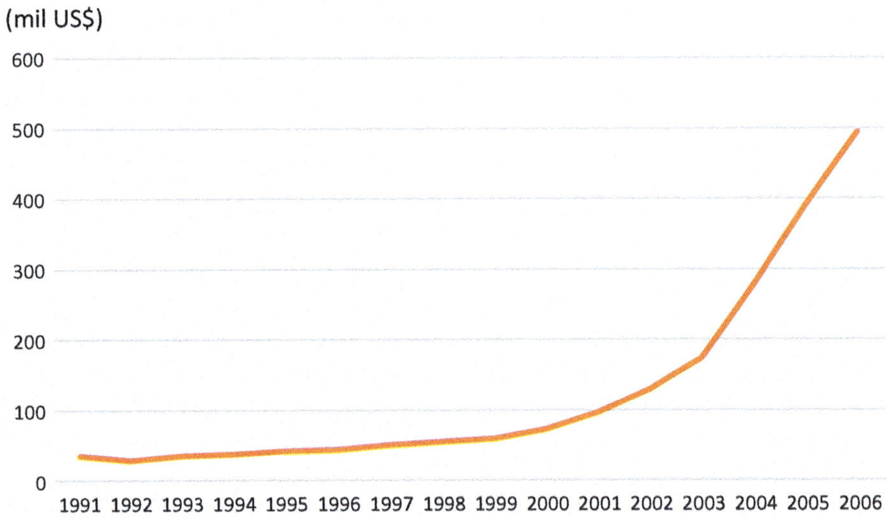

Fig. 5.8 R&D investments by Indian drug companies (1991–2006) (*Source*: Cheri Grace, Ref. [11], William Greence, Ref. [12])

the same level and remain simple generics manufacturing businesses. This study decided to analyze each company's R&D investment.

Figure 5.9 shows four leading Indian pharmaceutical companies' R&D investments between 1998 and 2008 [13].

As mentioned, R&D investments tend to fluctuate due to a variety of factors such as business climate, financial results, and R&D strategies. However, all four leading Indian pharmaceutical companies plotted in Fig. 5.9 expanded their R&D expenditures significantly during the period.

As will be described in a later chapter, some Indian pharmaceutical companies constructed new R&D centers, while some others set up subsidiary companies exclusively for new drug development. Those capital investments helped to push up the amount of their R&D investment.

Dr. Reddy's shrank its R&D investment between 2005 and 2006. The company's annual report noted that, since sales revenues and profits were down in 2005 over the previous year, it was decided to employ a "smart R&D" strategy in 2006. This involved reducing R&D expenditure by narrowing down the number of research projects and increasing collaboration with other companies. Dr. Reddy's sales/profit returned to the previous levels in the following year [7].

A research consulting firm, Espicom Business Intelligence, reported that some Indian companies had initiated development of NCEs, taking advantage of the TRIPS Agreement and introduction of product patents in 2005 [14].

According to Yuji Watanabe, out of the total R&D investment by the Indian pharmaceutical industry, 30% went into new drug (NCE) development and the remaining 70% into development of generics [15].

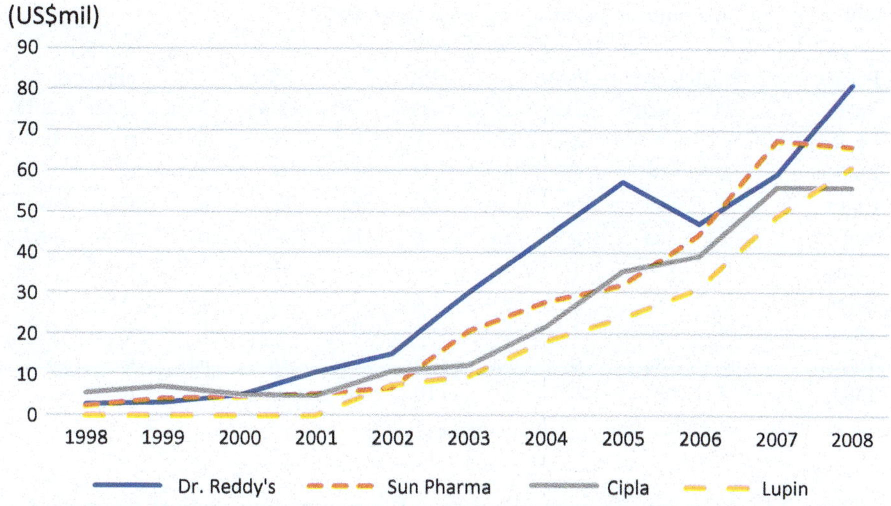

Fig. 5.9 R&D expenditure of leading Indian firms (*Source*: Gulshan Akhtar, Ref. [13])

Of the generics development expenditure, 43% (30% of total R&D expenditure) was directed to formulation development and the other 57% (40% of total R&D expenditure) into API development. Of the formulation development expenditure, 60% (18% of total R&D investment) went into conventional formulation development and the remaining 40% (12% of total R&D investment) into new development of new formulations such as drug delivery systems DDS [15].

5.5 Development Pipeline Analysis

A drug development pipeline is a set of drug candidates that a pharmaceutical company has under discovery or development at a given point in time. Since generic manufacturers are not required to conduct rigorous clinical trials, they do not have pipelines. Having a development pipeline is deemed to be proof that a company is engaging in new drug development. The progress of new drug development activity by a particular company can be understood by analyzing its development pipelines.

As mentioned above, until the mid-1990s, all Indian pharmaceutical companies exclusively manufactured and sold generic drugs. At that time, no Indian companies were engaged in new drug development; hence, none of them had any new drug development pipelines.

However, from around the mid-1990s, some major Indian pharmaceutical companies began pouring big sums into R&D and initiating new drug development programs. As a result of their efforts, the major Indian pharmaceutical companies have their own drug development pipelines, which they have been strengthening. Some are even engaged in late-stage clinical trials, such as Phase II or Phase III trials.

Table 5.2 Pipelines of major Indian companies 2006 vs. 2016

Phases	Preclinical		PI		PII		PIII		Market approval	
Year	2006	2016	2006	2016	2006	2016	2006	2016	2006	2016
Dr. Reddy's	10	2	4	0	3	0	0	1	0	0
Ranbaxy	6	0	3	0	0	1	0	0	0	1
Cipla	0	na	0	na	0	na	0	na	0	na
Sun	3	na	0	na	2	na	0	na	0	na
Piramal	0	3	1	1	1	2	0	0	0	0
Zydus	3	1	2	4	2	1	0	2	0	0
Lupin	0	2	1	1	2	2	1	1	0	0
Torrent	6	na	0	na	0	na	0	na	0	na
Total	28	8	11	6	10	6	1	4	0	1

Source: Business Insights, Ref. [16], R. Joseph, Ref. [17]

Table 5.2 shows development pipelines of Indian pharmaceutical companies as of 2006 and 2016 [16, 17].

On October 21, 2013, Ranbaxy (now Sun Pharmaceutical) announced that it had received approval from the Indian government's Central Drugs Standard Control Organization (CDSCO) to manufacture and market Synriam for treatment of uncomplicated malaria in adults. That drug became India's first new chemical entity (NCE).

5.6 Analysis of Patent Applications in India

Next, this study decided to analyze the trend of patent applications by the Indian pharmaceutical industry. As a result of R&D activity, intellectual property is produced. IP management is the key to business success. As mentioned above (Sect. 2.2), product patent protection is vital for the pharmaceutical business. Obtaining IP, especially product patents, represents a major step on the path to success [18].

In fact, Indian pharmaceutical companies had been filing patent applications over a long period. As mentioned above, India has a long history of patent protection. However, under the Patents Act, 1970, only process patents were protected in the pharmaceutical field, not product patents. After some major Indian pharmaceutical companies started launching new drug development programs in the mid-1990s, they began increasing the number of patent applications in order to protect their IP [18].

Figure 5.10 shows the trend of patent applications [19].

The number of patent applications remained under 10,000 in the 1990s. The figure rapidly increased in the 2000s.

In the figure, the horizontal axis shows the year of patent application, the year in which examination commenced and the year in which a patent was granted.

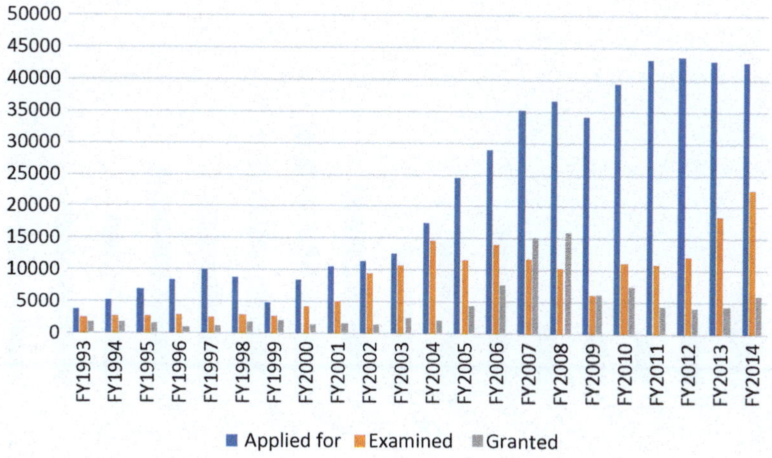

Fig. 5.10 Patents applied for/examined/granted in India (*Source*: Indian Patent Office Annual Report (FY1993-FY2015))

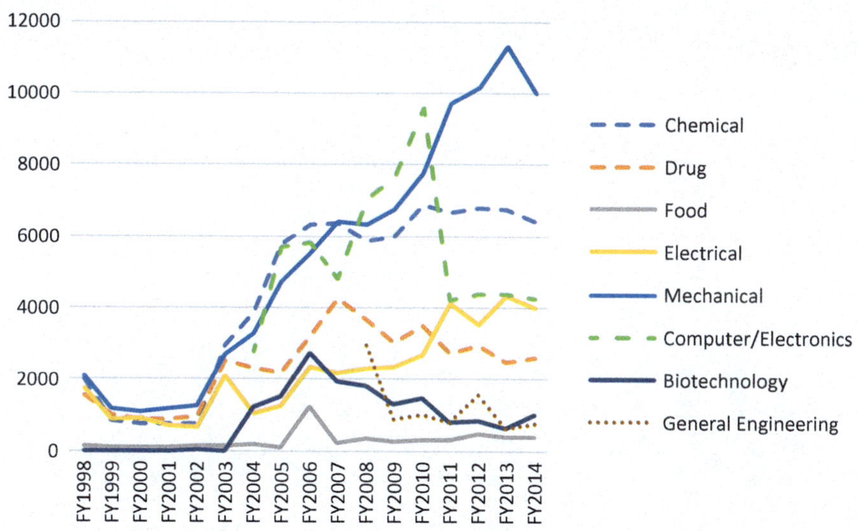

Fig. 5.11 Patent applications by field in India (*Source*: IPO Annual Report 1998–2015)

Figure 5.11 shows the number of patent applications by field.

When a patent application is filed, an IPO examiner categorizes the application into a field in accordance with International Patent Classification (IPC) #25 rules.

Figures 5.12 and 5.13 show the number of drug-related applications and patents granted [20].

IPO in FY2007 added a new category: "Bio Medical." Figures 5.12 and 5.13 include "Bio Medical" patent applications and patents granted.

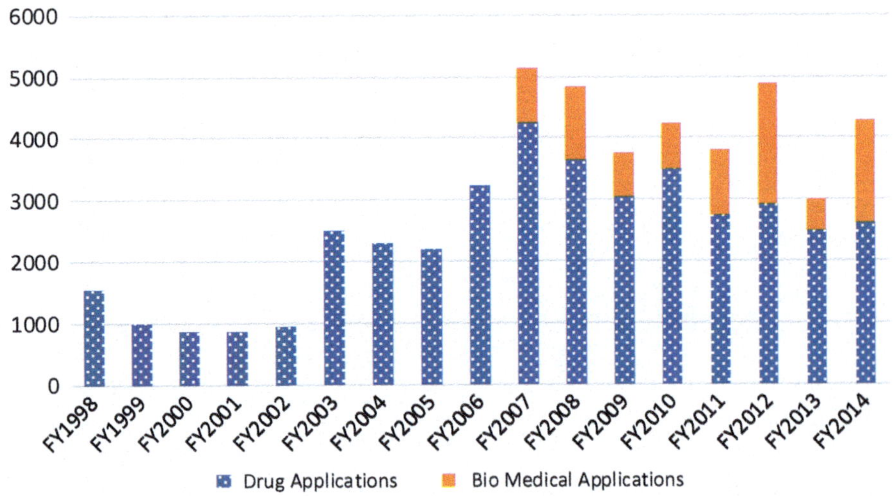

Fig. 5.12 Drug-related patent applications (FY1998-FY2014) (*Source*: IPO Annual Report FY1998-FY2015)

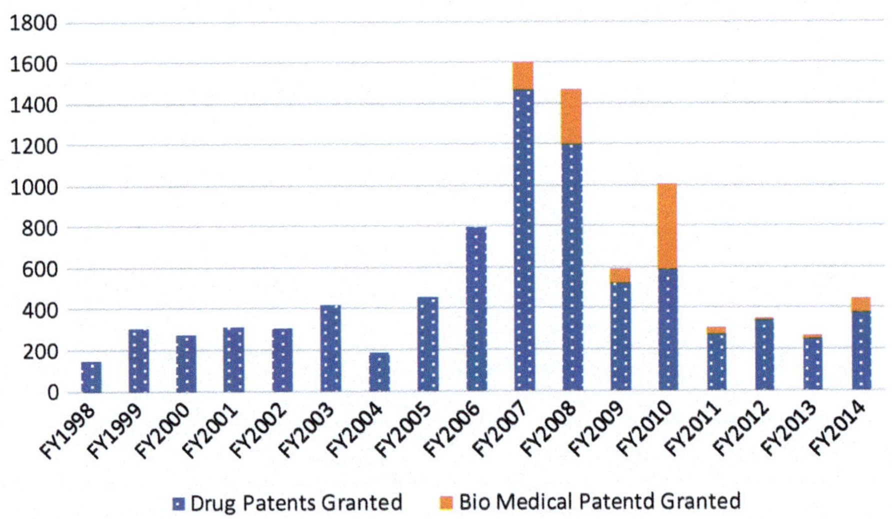

Fig. 5.13 Drug-related patents granted (FY1998-FY2014) (*Source*: IPO Annual Report FY1998-FY2015)

Each company decides whether or not to apply for a patent on a particular invention according to its own IP strategy. In order to analyze each company's patent applications trend, this study extracted patent application data from the IPO website using its internal search engine [20].

Figure 5.14 shows the number of patent applications by major pharmaceutical companies.

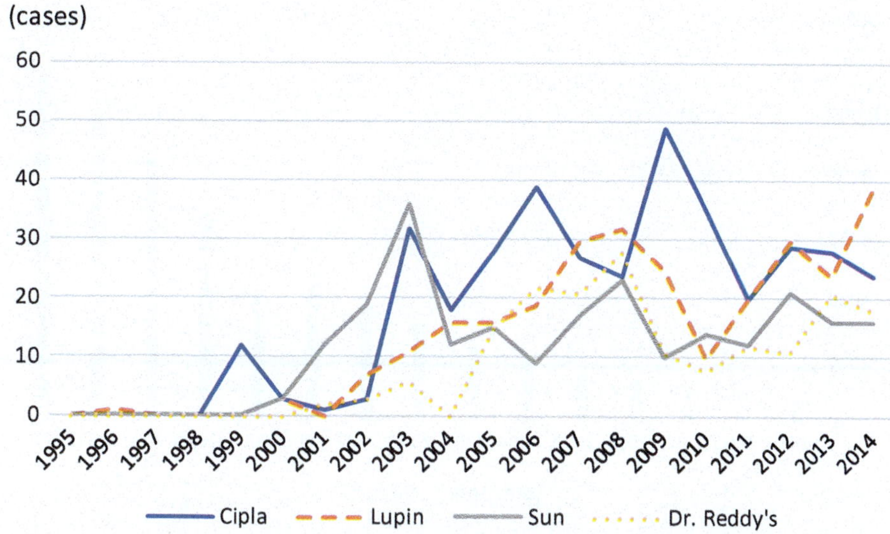

Fig. 5.14 The number of patent applications by major Indian pharmaceutical companies

In India, a patent application filed with the IPO will become publicly accessible in 18 months. Figure 5.14 indicates that the number of patent applications being filed by major Indian pharmaceutical companies has increased since the beginning of the 2000s.

5.7 An Analysis of Medical Products Trade (Bulk/Intermediates and Formulations)

As the sixth indicator, this study analyzed trade data, including both bulk/intermediates and formulations.

As mentioned above, it is believed that the Indian government inserted the Section 3 (d) into the Patents (Amendment) Act, 2005 in order to prevent penetration of the Indian market by foreign-owned pharmaceutical companies.

In this category, this study first analyzed import/export data for all medical products.

Prior to introduction of product patents in India, some stakeholders, such as industry associations, international NGOs/NPOs, and patient communities, raised objections, arguing that if product patents were to be introduced, (a) foreign goods and products would rapidly enter the Indian market and (b) Indian pharmaceutical companies might have difficulty exporting their goods and products to other countries.

According to TradeEconomics.com, India's pharmaceutical export grew from US$855.9 million in 1999 to US$11.1 billion in 2013, while the country's

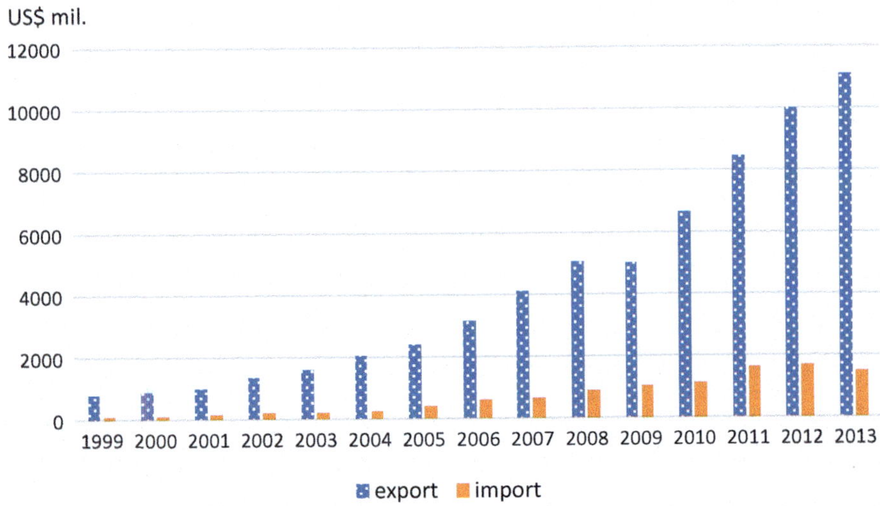

Fig. 5.15 India exports and imports of pharmaceutical products (*Source*: Ministry of Commerce & Industry, Ref. [21])

Fig. 5.16 Destinations for Indian pharmaceutical products by region

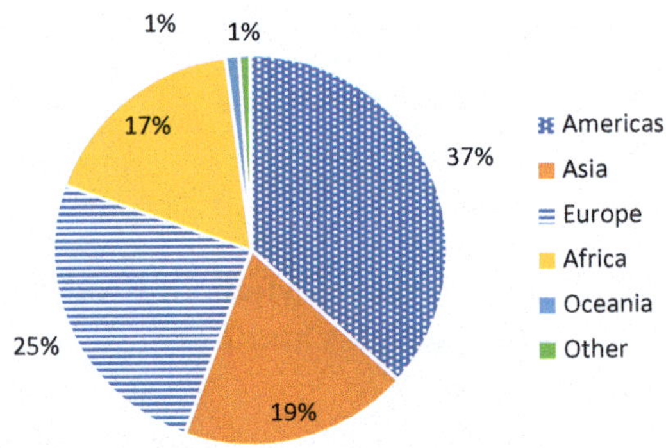

pharmaceutical import grew from US$138.6 million in 1999 to US$1.55 billion in 2013. The original data comes from Ministry of Commerce and Industry of India [21].

Since 1999, both exports and imports have expanded. However, exports grew by a much higher percentage than imports.

Figure 5.15 shows India exports and imports of pharmaceutical products (1999–2013).

According to IBEF, India now exports its products to 200 countries and is the world's largest supplier of generic drugs, accounting for 20% of global generic drug exports (in terms of volume), and the US market is the major export destination for Indian generic pharmaceutical products [22].

The leading destinations for Indian formulations used to be Russia and the CIS (Commonwealth of Independent States). However, as of 2015, the main destinations for Indian formulations are the US and other regulated markets [22].

Figure 5.16 shows destinations for Indian export products by region.

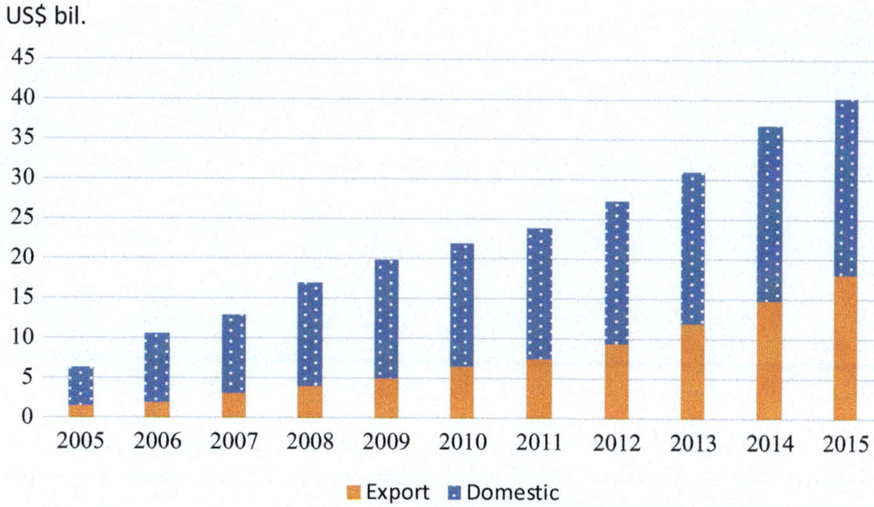

Fig. 5.17 Market values: export business vs. domestic business (*Source*: Ref. [24])

Table 5.3 Foreign business ratios of four leading Indian pharmaceutical companies

	Revenues FY2015 (Mil US$)	Domestic revenues (Mil US$)	Foreign revenues (Mil US$)	Ratio of Foreign revenues (%)
Dr. Reddy's	2,331	326	2,005	86
Lupin	1,981	476	1,505	76
Sun	3,415	649	2,766	81
Cipla	1,787	697	1,090	61

Source: Ref. [25]

The Americas (mostly the US) account for 37%, followed by Europe, Asia, and Africa.

Naturally, a large share of revenues comes from export business. Figure 5.17 shows export revenues vs. domestic revenues for the Indian pharmaceutical industry [23]. According to Fig. 5.17, export business accounted for 25% of total market value in 2005. In 2015, the export proportion increased to 47% [24].

The four leading Indian pharmaceutical companies selected for analysis in this study are all heavily reliant on export business. Table 5.3 shows the ratios of foreign business for those four Indian companies [25].

Compared to the steep increase in exports, imports of pharmaceutical products into India have maintained a steady growth rate.

Prior to introduction of product patents, some stakeholders raised objections, arguing that once product patents were introduced in India, foreign products would rapidly enter the Indian market and would eventually dominate it.

However, so far, at least, that has not happened. According to IBEF (Jan. 2017), patented drugs account for 9% of the Indian pharmaceutical market. The current

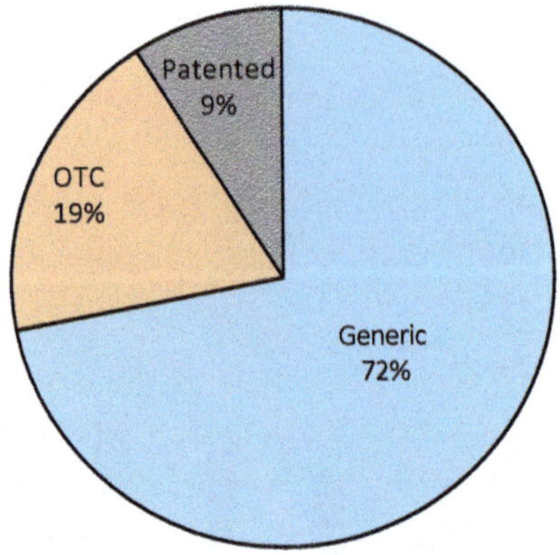

Fig. 5.18 Market share of Indian drug market by segment (*Source*: IBEF, Ref. [26])

status of the Indian pharmaceutical industry compiled by the Japan Pharmaceutical Manufacturers Association (JPMA) noted that only nine brand-name drugs (patented drugs) had entered the Indian market.

5.8 Development Model of Indian Pharmaceutical Industry

In order to further understand the Indian pharmaceutical industry's business development, this study decided to examine leading Indian pharmaceutical companies' business performances, transition of business model, and change of company organization, referring to each company's annual report and other relevant materials.

Dr. Arun Sawhney, API Business Department President for Dr. Reddy's, at the 2007 JETRO BioLink Forum in Tokyo, suggested that Indian pharmaceutical companies will evolve from the initial "wait and see" position, to "vendor-based outsourcing," to "build-operate-transfer for selected activities," to "partnerships for end-to-end research," and, finally, to "Captive R&D Centers." [27] (Fig. 5.19).

Some prior studies, including Chaturvedi & Chataway and Kale & Little, described how Indian pharmaceutical companies changed their business models, taking advantage of the TRIPS Agreement in 1995 and introduction of product patents in 2005, and began developing value-added generic drugs and/or new drugs (NCEs) [28, 29].

Bloomberg Businessweek on April 18, 2005, reported that India had more than 50 pharmaceutical research centers and more were expected (to be built) in the reported year (2005) "because, after a new patent protection law was enacted, Indian companies could no longer ignore the patents of multinational drug companies and produce unlicensed generics as Indian firms had done for 30 years." The magazine quoted Dr. Swati A. Piramal, then director of the Piramal Center, as saying: "Indian companies are no longer going to be just copycats; we want to take our rightful place at the top table with the developed countries" [30].

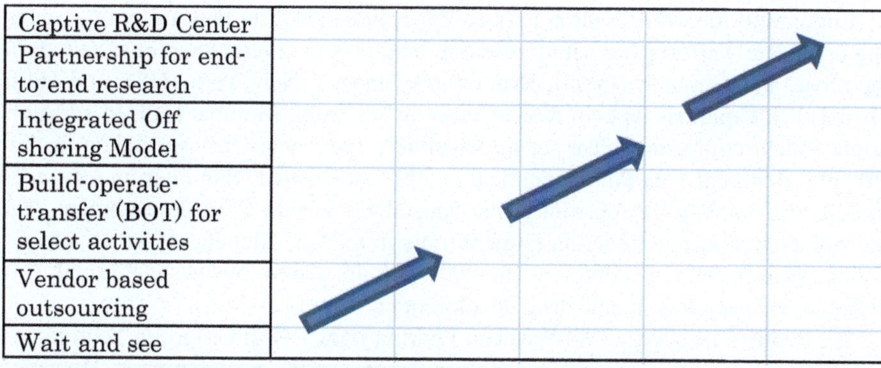

Fig. 5.19 Business model evolution of Indian pharmaceutical companies (*Source*: Ref. [27])

Several Indian pharmaceutical companies' annual reports featured declarations of determination.

Dr. Reddy's annual report carried a mission statement: "Becoming a discovery-led global pharmaceutical company." In 1994, in line with that statement, Dr. Reddy's became the first Indian pharmaceutical company to initiate a new drug discovery program. Since then, the company has increased R&D investment and strengthened its drug development pipelines [7].

Taking another tack, Lupin featured the slogan "Becoming an Innovation-led Transnational Pharmaceutical Company" in its annual report. The company has focused on R&D since the mid-2000s. In FY2016, it poured 16 billion Rp., or 11.7% of its sales revenue, into R&D [8].

Sun Pharmaceutical, the largest pharmaceutical company in India following its acquisition of Ranbaxy, has had a particular focus on the US market. Since the mid-2000s, Sun has been conducting clinical trials in that market. As will be discussed later, Sun set up a subsidiary company that specializes in NCE development [9].

Cipla's vision is to be a global pharmaceutical company "whose goal is to ensure that no patient shall be denied access to high-quality and affordable medicines and support." In line with that commitment, Cipla set up two spin-off companies in 2016: Cipla Health Limited, a consumer healthcare company, and Cipla BioTec, a biosimilar company [10].

As mentioned above, Dr. Arun Sawhney of Dr. Reddy's suggested in a Tokyo seminar that Indian companies will evolve from a "wait and see" position, to "vendor-based outsourcing," to "build-operate-transfer for selected activities," to "partnerships for end-to-end research," and, finally, to "Captive R&D Center" [27].

Major Indian pharmaceutical companies would appear to have already attained the "goal" of the Sawhney model.

Dr. Reddy's has set up its own research institutes for development of new drugs (NCEs) in Hyderabad and Bangalore, Cambridge (UK), Princeton (US), and the Netherlands [7].

Lupin built its own Research Park in Pune, India [8]. Sun Pharmaceutical, gearing up its R&D efforts, has set up research institutes in several locations: Vadodara, Mumbai, and Gurgaon (India); Brampton (Canada); New York (US); and Haifa (Israel) [9]. Cipla has its own R&D Center in Vikhroki, Mumbai [10]. In addition, some Indian companies have set up subsidiary companies that specialize in new drug development. Sun Pharmaceutical in 2007 established "Sun Pharma Advanced Research Company," a subsidiary that specializes in new drug development. The subsidiary has been conducting clinical trials in the US. Nicholas Piramal, a major Indian pharmaceutical company, in 2008 set up a new business, Piramal Life Science, to specialize in new drug development.

Dr. Reddy's in 2006 set up Perlecan Pharma jointly with Citigroup Venture and CICI Venture and transferred four new molecules to the new company. However, Perlecan Pharma failed to develop those molecules. Following failure of the business, the company was shut down.

5.9 Summary of This Chapter

This chapter undertook first-step analysis in line with the analytical framework described in Chap. 3. This chapter analyzed a variety of indicators that reflect Indian pharmaceutical industry activities. It also analyzed the behavior and actions of the Indian pharmaceutical industry in the wake of enforcement of the TRIPS Agreement in 1995 and introduction of product patents in 2005 and the kinds of outcomes that resulted from that behavior and those actions.

From prior studies, it was shown that, when more stringent patent protection is introduced in a developing country, it tends to cause economic loss. India is categorized as a developing country. In order to clarify the impact of product patents on the Indian economy, this study analyzed six indicators: stock prices, business performance, R&D investment, R&D pipelines, patent application data, and trade data. As stated earlier, analysis of these six indicators showed that the Indian pharmaceutical industry continued to enjoy strong and healthy growth, even after 2005.

Indian data are sometimes incomplete and tend to have different bases. In order to compensate for such issues, the author of this study decided to carry out a series of on-site interviews with stakeholders. The next chapter describes those analyses.

References

1. S. La Croix and A. Kawaura, "Product Patent Reform and Its Impact on Korea's Pharmaceutical Industry," *International Economic Journal* 10, no. 1 (1996): 109–124.
2. The Office of the Controller General of Patents, Designs, & Trade Marks (CGPDTM) Website, http://www.ipindia.nic.in/index.htm.

3. The National Stock Exchange (NSE) Website, http://www.nseindia.com.
4. H. Bhojwani, "Developing Innovation Capacity in India" (paper submitted to The Centre for the Management of Intellectual Property in Health Research and Development, 2005): 7.
5. Visiongain, "Indian Pharmaceutical Market Outlook 2009–2024 (2009): 32.
6. METI, "FY2016 Medical Technology, Service Center Promotion Program, Medical International Expansion Country Report: India" (March 2017): 55. Original data: Espicom, "Worldwide Pharmaceutical Market Forecasts to 2019" (2014).
7. Dr. Reddy's, "Annual Reports," http://www.drreddys.com/investors/reports-and-filings/annual-reports.
8. Lupin, "Annual Reports," http://www.lupin.com/archives-annual-report.php.
9. Sun Pharma, "Annual Reports," http://www.sunpharma.com/investors/annualreports.
10. Cipla, "Annual Reports," http://www.cipla.com/en/investor-information/annual-report-and-chairman-s-speech.html.
11. Cheri Grace, "The Effect of Changing Intellectual Property on Pharmaceutical Industry Prospects in India and China: Considerations for Access to Medicines," *DFID Health Systems Resource Centre* (June 2004): 37.
12. William Greene, "The Emergence of India's Pharmaceutical Industry and Implications for the U.S. Generic Drug Market" (Office of Economics working paper, no. 2007-05-A, U.S. International Trade Commission, May 2007): 15.
13. Gulshan Akhtar, "Indian Pharmaceutical Industry: An Overview," *IOSR Journal of Humanities and Social Science* 13, no. 3 (Jul. – Aug. 2013): 58.
14. "India World Pharmaceutical Market Q2 2010," *Espicom Business Intelligence* (2010): 54.
15. Yuji Watanabe, "Pharmaceutical Intellectual Property Protection in India" (report, TRIPS Study Group, Institute for International Trade and Investment, 2009: 37, https://www.jpo.go.jp/cgi/link.cgi?url=/shiryou/toushin/chousa/trips_chousa_houkoku.htm.
16. Business Insights, "The Indian Pharmaceutical Market to 2011" (2007).
17. R. Joseph, "Pharmaceutical Industry and Public Policy in Post-reform India" (Routledge India, 2016).
18. Hiroyuki Odagiri, *Economics of Biotechnology* (Toyo Keizai Inc., 2006), 284.
19. Annual Report of the Office of the Controller General of Patents, Designs and Trade Marks, Department of Industrial Policy & Promotion, Ministry of Commerce & Industry, Government of India, FY1993-FY2015. http://www.ipindia.nic.in/annual-reports-ipo.htm.
20. Indian Patent Office Website Search Engine, The Office of the Controller General of Patents, Designs, Trade Marks and Geographical Indication, Government of India Website, http://www.ipindia.nic.in.
21. Ministry of Commerce & Industry, Tradingeconomics.com, http://www.tradingeconomics.com/india/exports-of-pharmaceutical-products.
22. IBEF, "Pharmaceuticals" (Jan. 2017): 13.
23. "GMR Data: The Indian Pharmaceutical Market – Leading Domestic Companies" (2015): 41.
24. "GMR Data: The Indian Pharmaceutical Market – Leading Domestic Companies" (2015): 38.
25. "GMR Data: The Indian Pharmaceutical Market – Leading Domestic Companies" (2015): 46.
26. IBEF, "Pharmaceuticals" (June 2017): 11.
27. Arun Sawhney, "Business Models and Partnering Strategies in Asia's Emerging Biotech Market" (presentation, JETRO BioLink Forum 2007 "Connecting the BioTech World," Pacifico Yokohama, Yokohama, Japan, Sept. 19–21, 2007): 12.
28. Kalpana Chaturvedi and Joanna Chataway, "Strategic Integration of Knowledge in Indian Pharmaceutical Firms: Creating Competencies for Innovation," *International Journal of Business Innovation and Research* 1, no. 1/2 (2006): 27–50.

29. Dinar Kale et al., "Reconfiguration of Competencies for Innovation: The Case of the Indian Pharmaceutical Industry" (presentation at a conference in honor of Keith Pavitt, Open University Business School, Nov. 13–15, 2003).
30. Manjeet Kripalani, "India: Bigger Pharma" (interview with Dr. Swati A. Piramal, Bloomberg Businessweek, April 18, 2005).

Chapter 6
Analysis of Patents Act Enforcement After Introduction of Product Patents

This chapter describes the second-step analysis—on the roles of the Indian government—conducted according to the research framework described in Chap. 3. In order to determine if Section 3 (d) of the Patents (Amendment) Act, 2005 provided protection for the Indian pharmaceutical industry and paved the way for the strong business performances of Indian pharmaceutical companies, the author visited India and conducted a series of interviews with various stakeholders, including pharmaceutical industry associations, major pharmaceutical companies, government offices, public research institutes, universities, law firms, and consulting firms.

6.1 Method of Analysis: Outlines of On-Site Interviews in India

As mentioned at the end of Chap. 5, Indian data is not always comprehensive. Sometimes, data with different bases are mixed together. There was some concern that the author might not be able to obtain comprehensive data on relationships between the Patents (Amendment) Act, 2005 and the results of data analysis and on relationships between Section 3 (d) and the results of data analysis. In order to address this issue, it was decided to conduct a series of on-site interviews with stakeholders in India.

The first round of on-site interviews was conducted between September 2007 and July 2009. A second round (follow-up study) was conducted between 2011 and 2015.

Sites visited: Pharmaceutical industry associations, Indian government offices including the Indian Patent Office, public research institutes, universities, law firms, and consulting firms. The author asked questions regarding the impacts of the Patents (Amendment) Act, 2005 and Section 3 (d).

Y. Mitsumori, *The Indian Pharmaceutical Industry*,
SpringerBriefs in Health Care Management and Economics,
https://doi.org/10.1007/978-981-10-6790-7_6

Interviews were conducted with the following organizations/firms:
Indian pharmaceutical industry associations:

- Indian Drug Manufacturers' Association (IDMA)
- Indian Pharmaceutical Alliance (IPA)
- Organisation of Pharmaceutical Producers of India (OPPI)

Major pharmaceutical companies in India:

- Ranbaxy
- Dr. Reddy's
- Lupin
- Sun Pharmaceutical
- Cipla

Indian government offices:

- Council of Scientific and Industrial Research (CSIR)
- Department of Biotechnology (DOB)
- Department of Science and Technology (DST)

Public research institutes:

- Indian Institute of Chemical Technology (IICT)
- Central Drug Research Institute (CDRI)

Universities:

- Indian Institutes of Technology (IIT)
- West Bengal National University of Juridical Sciences (NUJS)

Law firms/consulting firms:

- Corporate Group
- Shardul Amarchand Mangaldas
- Anand and Anand
- Lakshmikumaran & Sridharan
- Evalueserve
- K&S Partners

6.1.1 Pharmaceutical Industry Associations

There are several pharmaceutical industry associations in India. The three major ones are the Indian Drug Manufacturers' Association (IDMA), Indian Pharmaceutical Alliance (IPA), and Organisation of Pharmaceutical Producers of India (OPPI). IDMA is an association of small to medium-sized Indian pharmaceutical companies. IPA was set up by leading Indian pharmaceutical companies. OPPI was founded by foreign-owned pharmaceutical companies [1–3].

Reflecting the types of companies comprising their respective memberships, these three organizations hold differing positions regarding the Patents (Amendment) Act, 2005 and Section 3 (d).

In short, IDMA and IPA support the Patents (Amendment) Act, 2005 and Section 3 (d); OPPI takes an opposing position.

The author visited these three pharmaceutical industry associations and conducted a series of interviews with relevant persons regarding their respective organizations' stances on the Patents (Amendment) Act, 2005 and Section 3 (d).

6.1.2 *Pharmaceutical Industry in India*

According to JETRO, there are some 20,000 pharmaceutical companies in India [4].

Most are small- to medium-sized companies. Furthermore, only a small number of major Indian pharmaceutical companies are in a position to invest large sums of money in R&D activities and initiation of new drug development.

Major pharmaceutical companies in India include Dr. Reddy's, Lupin, Sun Pharmaceutical, Cipla, Aurobindo, Cadila, and Wockhardt. Ranbaxy was formerly the local industry leader, but it was purchased by Daiichi Sankyo Co., Ltd. in 2008 and subsequently acquired by Sun Pharmaceutical in 2014.

Among foreign-owned pharmaceutical companies, only GSK commanded a significant share of the Indian market as of 2005. GSK was the sole foreign-owned company to remain in India following enactment of the Patents Act, 1970. Since the 1970s, GSK has managed to maintain a successful business operation in India by employing low pricing strategies.

The author of this study conducted a series of interviews with major Indian companies, including Dr. Reddy's, Sun Pharmaceutical, Cipla, Lupin, Wockhardt, Aurobindo, and with GSK, the only foreign-owned company with significant market share in India. The author also visited Blue Cross Laboratories, which is headed by a former executive director of IDMA, and Japanese pharmaceutical companies, such as Eisai Co., Ltd., Astellas Pharma Inc., and Daiichi Sankyo India Pharma.

Through the series of interviews, this study collected information about companies' business strategies in the post-TRIPS era and the impact of the Patents (Amendment) Act, 2005.

6.1.3 *Indian Government*

The Indian Patent Office (Office of the Controller General of Patents, Designs and Trade Marks) has four offices across India: Mumbai, New Delhi, Kolkata, and Chennai. Each office independently carries out examination of patent applications.

The Indian government, in order to promote science and technology in India, set up the Council of Scientific and Industrial Research (CSIR). The CSIR has 38 research institutes across India, covering almost all science fields.

The author visited Indian Patent Offices (in New Delhi, Mumbai and Kolkata), CSIR headquarters in New Delhi, and two research institutes operated by CSIR (IICT and CDRI) and collected information about their positions regarding the Indian IP regime and opinions on the Patents (Amendment) Act, 2005 and Section 3 (d).

6.1.4 *Universities*

There are many universities in India.

The Indian Institutes of Technology (IIT) is reputed to be one of the country's top academic institutions. The author visited IIT's Mumbai Campus and the West Bengal National University of Juridical Sciences (NUJS), one of India's leading law schools in Kolkata to collect opinions from professors regarding the Patents (Amendment) Act, 2005 and Section 3 (d).

The interviewee at NUJS, Prof. Basheer, is a prominent scholar and expert on the Patents (Amendment) Act, 2005 and Section 3 (d). His article is cited in Chap. 4 of this book.

6.1.5 *Law Firms and Consulting Firms*

There are many law firms and consulting firms in India. The author visited Corporate Group (New Delhi), Evalueserve (New Delhi), Shardul Amarchand Mangaldas (Mumbai), Lakshmikumaran & Sridharan (New Delhi), and Anand and Anand (New Delhi).

Through their business activities, these law firms and consulting firms are in a position to accumulate a great deal of information about Indian patent law and progressive changes. These specialists' opinions are especially valuable because of their neutral status, i.e., their independence from government agencies and industry.

The author sought their opinions from a neutral perspective regarding the Patents (Amendment) Act, 2005 and Section 3 (d).

6.2 Views of Pharmaceutical Industry and the Indian Government

In order to examine the impact of Section 3 (d), this part (Sect. 6.2) quotes the results of a series of interviews with Indian pharmaceutical industry associations regarding the Patents (Amendment) Act, 2005 and Section 3 (d).

This part (Sect. 6.2) also quotes an interview with a government officer aimed at clarifying the intent of the Indian government in inserting Section 3 (d) into the Patents (Amendment) Act, 2005.

6.2.1 IDMA

IDMA, established in 1961, is an association of small- to medium-sized pharmaceutical companies. As of January 2017, it has 900 member companies, which together command 75% of the market for formulations and 85% of bulk/intermediates business in India.

When the Indian government was engaged in revising its patent law in the early 2000s, the IDMA cooperated on the task and helped with the drafting of Section 3 (d). In other words, Section 3 (d) was the outcome of joint efforts by the Indian government and IDMA.

In an interview with the author, Dr. Gajanan Wakankar, then Executive Director of IDMA, said: "Since Section 3 (d) prevents foreign-owned pharmaceutical companies from obtaining patent protection with their trivial improvements, Indian pharmaceutical companies are able to keep producing generic drugs. If the Patents (Amendment) Act, 2005 did not contain Section 3 (d), foreign-owned companies could get patent protection for their trivial improvements and then Indian manufacturers would have to stop producing generic drugs."

Dr. Wakankar suggested that, based on Section 3 (d), the Indian Patent Office rejects patent applications for trivial improvements submitted by foreign-owned companies, and, consequently, Indian pharmaceutical companies are able to keep manufacturing generics.

In an interview with the author, Dr. Nichal H. Israni, chairman of Blue Cross Laboratories (a former president of IDMA), asked "Why do we need to think about brand-name drugs (patented drugs) when Indian people cannot afford essential medicines? The Indian government has an obligation to fight poverty. Currently, the most important challenge for the Indian government is ensuring that the general public has greater access to generic drugs." He suggested that the Indian government had formulated its intellectual property policies (including patent law) based on the need to improve Indian people's access to generic drugs.

Regarding Section 3 (d) of the Patents (Amendment) Act, 2005, Dr. Israni referred to social issues such as "poverty," speaking from a perspective which is quite different from that of foreign-owned pharmaceutical companies.

6.2.2 IPA

The Indian Pharmaceutical Alliance, established in 1999, is an association of major Indian pharmaceutical companies which (1) command more than 1% of the Indian market, (2) pour large sums of money into R&D, and (3) have obtained marketing approval outside of India.

IPA has been engaging with a range of issues related to the pharmaceutical industry: dealing with intellectual property (patents) and public health, lobbying the Indian government, and providing the government with a variety of useful information to assist in policy-making.

In an interview with the author, Mr. D. G. Shah, Secretary General of IPA, said that the Patents (Amendment) Act, 2005 had two objectives: one was to secure access to medicines for the Indian general public; the other was to prevent evergreening.

He continued: "The Indian government and IPA worked together to create unique Indian patent laws which would achieve a balance between benefits for innovators and benefits for Indian consumers. We did not intend to imitate US or European patent laws."

Mr. Shah also stressed the importance of the consumer perspective and argued that it is important to find a balance between innovators' (pharmaceutical companies') benefits and consumers' benefits. This position is strikingly different from that of foreign-owned companies.

6.2.3 OPPI

OPPI, established in 1965, is an association of foreign-owned pharmaceutical companies operating in India. Its membership comprises companies that are pro-patents. Currently, 31 (as of May 2017) foreign-owned companies are members of the association.

Mr. Tapan Ray, then Director General of OPPI, said: "We have concerns about Section 3 (d) having been inserted into the Patents (Amendment) Act, 2005. We hope that the Indian government will take the necessary steps to deal with the problem (revise the law)."

OPPI argues that India should have a TRIPS-compatible patent law given that India was a founding member of the WTO.

Mr. Tapan Ray continued: "So long as India's patent law contains Section 3 (d), foreign-owned companies will decline to initiate R&D in the Indian market."

OPPI recognized that the existence of Section 3 (d) in Indian patent law has a negative impact on the business performance of foreign-owned companies, and it is hoping for removal of that section from the Patents (Amendment) Act, 2005.

6.2.4 CSIR

At CSIR, the author interviewed Mr. Naresh Kumar, then head of the R&D Planning Division. Referring to the Mashelkar Technical Expert Group (TEG) report of 2006, Mr. Kumar mentioned that one reason why the Patents (Amendment) Act, 2005 deviated from the TRIPS framework was that, when the government was working on revision of patent laws in around 2005, it came under strong pressure from Parliament, NGOs, and citizen groups.

Mr. Kumar said: "In India, the public and NGOs have a great deal of power. They want to purchase high-quality medicines at lower prices. If India were to introduce a more stringent patent regime equivalent to those in advanced countries, drug prices in India could rise sharply. Then, citizens and NGOs would be unhappy. That's why India was required to have policies that ensured access to inexpensive, high-quality medicines for the general public. There needed to be a certain loophole in the Indian system."

Mr. Kumar argued that, under pressure from NGOs and citizen groups, the Indian government decided to insert Section 3 (d) in order to protect the public interest.

This series of interviews suggested that, when a revision bill for the Indian patents act was being discussed in Parliament, the Indian pharmaceutical industry, which was concerned about the rapid penetration by foreign-owned companies into the Indian market, lobbied the government and requested insertion of some form of safeguard section into the revised patents act. The Indian government, recognizing the need to protect the local pharmaceutical industry against foreign-owned companies, decided to insert Section 3 (d) into the Patents (Amendment) Act, 2005.

Also, it was suggested that foreign-owned pharmaceutical companies, realizing that Section 3 (d) would have a negative impact on their business performance, sought elimination of Section 3 (d).

As shown by various data in Chap. 5, rapid penetration of the Indian pharmaceutical market by overseas-made products did not happen. So far, at least, Section 3 (d) has played the protectionist role envisaged by the Indian government.

6.3 Patent Rejection Based on Section 3 (d)

The Indian Patent Office has rejected a number of patent applications on the basis of Section 3 (d).

As mentioned above, Section 3 (d) strictly limits the scope of patentability and does not permit granting of patents for "derivatives" of known pharmaceutical substances unless they demonstrate enhanced efficacy.

As described in Sect. 2.4.1 ("Transition of Indian Patent Law"), when Novartis' Gleevec patent application was rejected, the issue was widely reported by mass media and became the subject of a major debate, not just in India but worldwide [5].

This section analyzes the Gleevec (Novartis) case.

6.3.1 Patent Rejection for Gleevec

In January 2006, the Chennai Patent Office examined a patent application for Gleevec and rejected it on two grounds: (1) lack of novelty and inventive steps because the 1993 patents had already claimed all pharmaceutical salt forms of imatinib and (2) on the basis of Section 3 (d) because the new product did not demonstrate enhanced efficacy [6].

This Novartis-Gleevec case attracted considerable attention, not just in India but worldwide, because (1) the Gleevec patent was approved in 40 countries; (2) Indian pharmaceutical companies were manufacturing several generic versions of patented drugs and selling them not only in India but also to Third World countries.

There was a major debate over the issue, involving the Indian government, the government of Switzerland (where Novartis' head office is located), developing countries, and international NGOs and NPOs which provide inexpensive Indian drugs to those countries.

Novartis appealed the rejection to the Madras High Court in May 2006. Its appeal was opposed by the Indian government, several generic drug companies, and an Indian NGO (the Cancer Patients Aid Association).

The Madras High Court took up the matters of TRIPS compliance and constitutionality, ultimately granting a judicial decision against Novartis on August 8, 2007. First, the court held that it lacked jurisdiction to review whether or not Section 3 (d) is TRIPS compliant. Second, the court decided that Section 3 (d) does not violate Article 14 of the Constitution of India [7].

The patent rejection case was sent to the IPAB, a special tribunal established in 2003 to hear challenges to patent rejections. The IPAB took up the matter of the patent office's rejection of the Gleevec patent application.

On June 26, 2009, the IPAB issued a decision overturning the Patent Controller's rejection of the application based on lack of novelty and inventive steps but upholding its findings as to Section 3 (d) [8].

In the wake of the IPAB decision, Novartis appealed to the Indian Supreme Court by filing a special leave petition challenging the IPAB's interpretation of Section 3 (d). The Supreme Court on April 1, 2013, upheld the rejection of the patent application (1602/MAS/1998) filed with the Indian Patent Office by Novartis for Gleevec in 1998 [9].

6.3.2 Roche vs. Cipla over Tarceva

Roche applied for granting of a patent for Tarceva (erlotinib) in March 1996. The Chennai Patent Office granted a patent for the anticancer drug in July 2007.

However, Cipla in December 2007 began manufacturing and marketing a generic version of Tarceva (erlotinib), claiming that the brand-name product's patent was invalid.

In January 2008, Roche initiated infringement proceedings against Cipla, seeking an interim injunction to suspend the Indian company's marketing of a generic version of Tarceva.

However, the Delhi High Court Single Bench in March 2008 rejected the interim injunction application filed by Roche.

In his judgment, S. R. Bhat, Single Bench Justice, noted:

"The Court cannot be unmindful of the right of the general public to access lifesaving drugs which are available and for which such access would be denied if the injunction were granted. The degree of harm in such eventuality is absolute; the chances of improvement of life expectancy, even chances of recovery in some cases, would be snuffed out altogether if the injunction were granted. Such injuries to third parties are non-compensable. Another way of viewing it is that, if the injunction in the case of a lifesaving drug were to be granted, the Court would in effect be stifling Article 21 so far as those who would have or could have access to Erlocip are concerned."

Roche appealed the case to the Division Bench. However, the Division Bench of Delhi High Court upheld the decision of the Single Bench.

The Division Bench also mentioned:

"That general public access in India to lifesaving drugs assumes great significance and the public interest in greater public access to a lifesaving drug would have to outweigh the public interest in granting an injunction to Roche."

Roche submitted a special leave petition to the Supreme Court. However, the Supreme Court dismissed the petition.

The main examination was separately brought to the Delhi High Court. The Delhi High Court in September 2012 determined that Roche's patent was not infringed by Cipla, although the Court admitted patentability of erlotinib. The court argued that both Tarceva, Roche's branded erlotinib drug, and Erlocip, Cipla's erlotinib drug, were the stable form of polymorph B; hence, the patent was rejected by the IPO on the basis of Section 3 (d) among other grounds.

Both Roche and Cipla appealed this case, and their appeals are presently pending before the Division Bench of the Delhi High Court [10].

6.4 Monetization of R&D Outcomes

The analysis in Chap. 5 showed that major Indian pharmaceutical companies began investing heavily in R&D and initiated new drug discovery/development programs. As shown in their pipelines, some large Indian pharmaceutical companies currently have molecules in late clinical trial stages, such as Phase II or Phase III. Recently, one India-originated NCE was successfully launched on the Indian market.

Besides NCE development, those major Indian pharmaceutical companies' efforts started to generate profits. This section describes three cases in which local pharmaceutical companies' R&D investments started contributing to the development of the Indian pharmaceutical industry—making profits—not in the form of new molecule launches but in different forms.

The first case is establishment of a subsidiary company specialized in new drug discovery/development. Several leading Indian pharmaceutical companies have set up such specialized subsidiaries, and some of them have started making money.

The second case is out-licensing. Some Indian pharmaceutical companies which initiated new drug discovery/development programs licensed out their molecules to third parties, and some of them succeeded in winning big licensing fees from partnering companies.

The third case is development of value-added generics. Many Indian pharmaceutical companies have recently begun focusing on development of novel drug delivery systems (DDS).

The following three sections describe these three cases.

6.4.1 New Subsidiaries for New Drug Discovery/Development

Sun Pharmaceutical, the largest pharmaceutical company in India, founded a subsidiary to specialize in new drug discovery and development. That subsidiary, Sun Pharma Advanced Research Company (SPARC), is running several DDS programs as well as a couple of NCE programs in the anticancer and anti-inflammatory drug fields.

The aim of establishing the new subsidiary was to hedge against risk; by separating high-risk business such as new drug development from the main business entity (Sun Pharmaceutical), the parent company could minimize risk in its primary business areas. SPARC had won approvals from US regulatory agencies and started selling products. The company is considered to be a successful case of capitalization of R&D investment.

Following Sun Pharmaceutical's success with SPARC, some other large Indian pharmaceutical companies also spun off new drug development companies. Dr. Reddy's set up a subsidiary for new drug development called Perlecan Pharma. Nicholas Piramal established a similar subsidiary, Piramal Life Science.

Dr. Reddy's, in cooperation with private equity investors ICICI Venture and Citigroup Venture Capital International Mauritius Limited, set up Perlecan Pharma and transferred four NCE assets to the new company. However, after failing to develop those four molecules, Perlecan Pharma was shut down.

Piramal Life Science in September 2014 shut down its drug discovery and research unit in Mumbai [11].

6.4.2 Out-Licensing

As mentioned above, it takes a long time and incurs high investment costs to develop a new drug. Especially in the late stage of development, a pharmaceutical company has to carry out large-scale clinical trials in which a great number of patient volunteers are involved. Naturally, late-stage clinical trials are very expensive.

Typically, when a small- to medium-sized pharmaceutical company is engaged in new drug discovery and development, it conducts only early-stage clinical trials in-house and then licenses out its molecule to a bigger pharmaceutical company for organization of later-stage clinical trials.

Compared to so-called mega pharma (the world's leading pharmaceutical companies), the scale of Indian pharmaceutical companies, even the biggest ones, is relatively small, and they have limited capital for investment compared to mega pharma companies. Accordingly, out-licensing of some molecules to other companies could be a solution to the problem of lack of capital for late-stage clinical trials.

Some of the big Indian pharmaceutical companies which have initiated new drug discovery/development programs have licensed their molecules to overseas manufacturers. The following section looks at two cases where Indian pharmaceutical companies have successfully out-licensed molecules and received substantial licensing fees.

1. Case of Glenmark

Glenmark, a leading Indian pharmaceutical company, had been aggressively licensing out its molecules and gaining cash flow from those deals.

In 2004, the company out-licensed Oglemilast, a PDE4 inhibitor, to a US pharmaceutical firm, Forest Laboratories, and received a total US$35 million in milestone payments.

The following year (2005), Glenmark concluded an agreement with a Japanese pharmaceutical company, Teijin Pharma, in respect of the same molecule. The deal could earn Glenmark a total US$53 million if the molecule cleared all development phases and were to be launched on the Japanese market.

In 2006, Glenmark out-licensed its Melogliptin to Merck Serono, a division of global drug major Merck KGaA, and received upfront payment of EUR25 million. The rights reverted to Glenmark in 2008 after Merck Serono decided to halt development due to refocusing of its portfolio (in 2008 Glenmark got back global rights for Melogliptin from Merck Serono).

In 2007, Glenmark out-licensed a painkiller molecule, GRC 6211, to Eli Lilly and received an upfront fee of US$45 million. (Glenmark announced in 2008 its partner Eli Lilly had suspended further clinical development for molecule GRC 6211).

2. Case of Dr. Reddy's

Dr. Reddy's was a pioneer in new drug development in India. It had developed several antidiabetic molecules and out-licensed some of them to foreign-owned companies.

In 1997, Dr. Reddy's out-licensed DRF 2593, an antidiabetic molecule, to Novo Nordisk for preclinical and clinical development. With that deal, Dr. Reddy's became the first Indian pharmaceutical company to out-license an original molecule.

In 1998, Dr. Reddy's out-licensed another antidiabetic molecule, DRF 2725, to Novo Nordisk.

In 2001, Dr. Reddy's out-licensed yet another antidiabetic molecule, DRF 4158, to Novartis. Those deals brought the company substantial financial returns. Dr. Reddy's deal with Novartis on DRF 4158 contained a package comprising US$55 million upfront plus milestone payments.

Unfortunately, further development of these three molecules was later terminated [12].

6.4.3 Drug Delivery Systems

Some Indian pharmaceutical companies have been placing emphasis on development of value-added generic drugs and particularly on development of DDS. They are frequently referred to as NDDS (Novel Drug Delivery Systems) in India.

As mentioned earlier, the Indian pharmaceutical industry had been allocating 12% of total investments to DDS (or NDDS) development [13].

DDS development has been actively pursued not just in India but worldwide.

Kamal Dua noted in his article on Pharmainfo.net that "DDS have a large number of advantages over conventional dosage forms, such as controlled and predictable release, lesser chance of dose dumping, reduction of frequency of administration, and minimization of side effects" [14].

An article appearing on a pharmaceutical industry website called Pharmabiz.com, titled "NDDS: New lease of life to an old molecule," reported that "a good number of firms in India have already identified NDDS as the future growth area" and pointed out that "Cipla, Ranbaxy, Wockhardt, Sun, JB Chemicals, and Ajanta Pharma have already made considerable progress on NDDS" [15].

A Japan Research Institute report noted that Dr. Reddy's, Cipla, and Lupin had been engaging in DDS research and development [16].

Furthermore, Indian pharmaceutical companies have concluded alliances with foreign-owned companies in relation to DDS technology.

Dr. Reddy's and a US-based pharmaceutical company, Aegis Therapeutics LLC, in January 2010 announced a partnership that would give Dr. Reddy's access to Aegis's Intravail drug delivery technology. The DDS products under this exclusive license agreement would be developed, manufactured, and marketed worldwide by

Dr. Reddy's. Aegis Therapeutics is a drug delivery technology company that commercializes its patented drug delivery and drug formulation technologies through product-specific licenses.

Dr. Reddy's also concluded an exclusive agreement with UK-based SkyePharma PLC to undertake a feasibility study on a product that utilized two of SkyePharma's proprietary drug delivery systems. SkyePharma has oral, inhalation, and topical drug delivery technology.

(In 2016 SkyePharma announced that it agreed to merge with Vectura, another UK-based pharmaceutical firm).

In addition, Dr. Reddy's concluded a partnering agreement with an Israeli company, SoluBest, on drug delivery technology. SoluBest's proprietary technology, the Solumer platform, is based on self-assembly of polymer compounds, creating highly stable particles. Under the agreement, Dr. Reddy's would develop a new, proprietary formulation of one of SoluBest's pipeline compounds.

Some leading Indian pharmaceutical companies have developed several DDS products, and sales revenues from them have contributed to robust growth for those companies.

6.5 Examination of Working Hypothesis

In Chap. 4, the author of this study set up a working hypothesis: Indian government effort—inserting the safeguarding clause Section 3 (d) in the Patents (Amendment) Act, 2005—and the Indian pharmaceutical industry's self-help efforts in changing its business model from a conventional purely generics business model to an integrated business model embracing both generic drugs (off-patent drugs) and brand-name drugs (patented drugs) created a synergistic effect which eventually mitigated the negative impact that a developing country would normally sustain in the wake of introduction of product patents.

Chapter 5 described a series of data analyses conducted in order to prove the working hypothesis.

To complement the data analyses described in Chap. 5, a series of interviews with various stakeholders, including pharmaceutical industry associations, government officials, university professors, and NGOs/NPOs, were conducted, and the results are described in this chapter.

These interviews revealed that the Indian government inserted Section 3 (d) into the Patents (Amendment) Act, 2005 with the intention of protecting the Indian pharmaceutical industry against foreign-owned companies.

By preventing foreign-owned companies from entering the Indian market, the Indian government sought:

1. To secure access to inexpensive, locally manufactured drugs for the Indian general public
2. To protect Indian pharmaceutical companies' generics business

3. To provide a grace period that would enable Indian pharmaceutical companies to develop value-added generic drugs and/or new drugs (patented drugs)

The Indian government decided to insert Section 3 (d) in order to achieve those objectives.

The following are the bases for this discussion:

1. Regarding the first discussion point, as shown in the court battle between Roche and Cipla over Tarceva, the Delhi High Court (single judge) declined Roche's request for a temporary injunction on the grounds of "public interest." The judge noted that availability of Cipla's lower-priced generic version would enable "greater access" to this lifesaving drug in India.
2. Regarding the second discussion point, an analysis in Sect. 5.7, "An Analysis of the Medical Products Trade (Bulk/Intermediates and Formulations)," showed that neither rapid entry into the Indian market by foreign-owned pharmaceutical companies nor a steep decline in exports of Indian pharmaceutical products had occurred thus far. On the other hand, an interview with IDMA in Sect. 6.2 ("Views of Pharmaceutical Industry and the Indian Government") showed that Section 3 (d) was inserted into the Patents (Amendment) Act, 2005 for the purpose of protecting Indian generic drug makers against foreign-owned companies.
3. Regarding the third discussion point, Sect. 5.5 "Development Pipeline Analysis" showed that major Indian pharmaceutical companies increased their R&D investments and initiated development of value-added generics and/or new drugs, taking advantage of TRIPS enforcement in 1995 and introduction of product patents in 2005. As a result, the development pipelines of these large Indian pharmaceutical companies were enhanced, and some Indian companies have molecules in late clinical trial stages, such as Phase II and Phase III.

   In 2012, Ranbaxy (now part of Sun Pharmaceutical), launched the anti-malaria drug, Synriam, India's first domestically developed drug. To date, there have been no other drugs developed and approved in India. Indian pharmaceutical companies do not yet have sufficient strength to resist the might of foreign-owned companies, and they need more time to reach the state where they can compete on an equal footing.

   The interview with a CSIR officer showed that the Indian government inserted Section 3 (d) in order to give Indian pharmaceutical companies time to develop NCEs and value-added drugs in order to compete with foreign-owned companies.

6.6 Discussion of Roles of Section 3 (d)

Upon enforcement of TRIPS in 1995, the Indian government in January 2005 revised its Patents Law, which is regarded as being TRIPS-compatible, and introduced product patents in the pharmaceutical and other fields. Prior studies showed that, when product patents are introduced in a developing country, that country's industrial development is impeded.

In fact, when enforcement of the TRIPS Agreement required India to introduce product patents by 2005, various stakeholders expressed concerns, asserting that introduction of product patents in India would have negative impacts on the Indian pharmaceutical industry.

Taking these objections into account, the Indian government inserted Section 3 (d) into the Patents (Amendment) Act, 2005 as part of its efforts to mitigate negative impacts.

Concurrently, the Indian pharmaceutical industry changed its business model from an exclusively generic drug production one to an integrated business model embracing both generic drugs and brand-name drugs.

This study set up a working hypothesis in Chap. 4: Indian government effort—inserting a safeguarding clause Section 3 (d) into Patents (Amendment) Act, 2005—and the Indian pharmaceutical industry's self-help efforts in changing its business model from the conventional exclusively generic drug production one to an integrated business model embracing both generic drugs (off-patent drugs) and brand-name drugs (patented drugs) created a synergistic effect which eventually mitigated the negative impacts that a developing country would normally sustain in the wake of introduction of product patents.

In order to examine this working hypothesis, this study first analyzed sales revenues and profits of major Indian pharmaceutical companies.

The analysis showed that Indian pharmaceutical companies continued to maintain robust growth even after introduction of product patents in 2005.

However, it is impossible for this study to conclude that introduction of Section 3 (d) into the Patents (Amendment) Act, 2005 was responsible for the robust development of the Indian pharmaceutical industry, even after introduction of product patents in 2005.

There could be several other reasons.

As a next step, the author of this study conducted a series of interviews in India with various stakeholders. Interviewees included pharmaceutical industry associations, pharmaceutical companies, government officers, lawyers, and public research institution researchers.

Those interviews revealed that:

1. The Indian government introduced Section 3 (d) in order to secure access by the Indian general public to inexpensive locally manufactured drugs.
2. Indian pharmaceutical companies continued to sell their products without losing market share to foreign-owned companies.
3. Given a grace period, the Indian pharmaceutical companies could develop value-added generic drugs and/or new drugs (patented drugs).

On the other hand, from an analysis of a variety of indicators for the Indian pharmaceutical industry in Chap. 5, it was found that Indian pharmaceutical companies increased R&D investment and initiated development of value-added generic and brand-name drugs. As a result, the major Indian pharmaceutical companies filed a greater number of patent applications and increased the number of molecules in their development pipelines.

This information and data showed that Indian pharmaceutical companies, working through industry associations, lobbied the Indian government for introduction of Section 3 (d).

However, those Indian Pharmaceutical companies also increased R&D investment, initiated development of value-added generic and brand-name drugs, and expanded their pipelines.

Indian pharmaceutical companies' change of business model—from the conventional reverse engineering model to an integrated business model embracing both generic drugs and brand-name drugs—played a role in enabling the industry to overcome the negative impacts of introduction of product patents and to continue to grow even after 2005.

In summary, Indian government policy—inserting Section 3 (d) in the Patents (Amendment) Act, 2005 to protect the Indian pharmaceutical industry—combined with the industry's self-efforts in changing business model from the conventional reverse engineering model to an integrated model embracing both generic drugs business and brand-name drugs business created a synergistic effect, and the Indian pharmaceutical industry continues to grow even after 2005.

Therefore, the working hypothesis was proved.

References

1. IDMA Website, http://www.idma-assn.org.
2. IPA Website, http://www.ipa-india.org.
3. OPPI Website, http://www.indiaoppi.com.
4. "A Report on Patent Enforcement in the Indian Pharmaceutical Industry," IP Department, JETRO New Delhi Office, (July 2013): 5.
5. Mika Yamana, "Pharmaceutical Industry and the Indian Patent Act with Particular Reference to Madras High Court's Novartis Rulings," *Patent Studies*, no. 44 (Sept. 2007): 37.
6. Dorothy Du, "Novartis Ag v. Union of India: 'Evergreening,' Trips, and 'Enhanced Efficacy' under Section 3 (d)," *Journal of Intellectual Property Law* 21, no. 2 (2014).
7. *W.P. Nos. 24759 and 24760 of 2006*, (decisions in the High Court of Judicature at Madras, Coram, the Hon'ble Mr. Justice R. Balasubramanian and the Hon'ble Mrs. Justice Prabha Sridevan, June 8, 2007), http://www.lawyerscollective.org/files/novartis/IIMadHC/Novartis%20AG%20v%20UoI%20and%20others%20[Mad%20HC%20judgment].pdf.
8. *Misc. Petition Nos. 1-5 of/2007 in TA/1-5/2007/PT/CH & Misc. Petition No. 33 of 2008 in TA/1/2007/PT/CH & TA/1-5/2007/PT/CH* (IPAB, Intellectual Property Appellate Board, June 26, 2009), http://www.lawyerscollective.org/files/novartis/IIIIPAB/Novartis%20AG%20v.%20UoI%20and%20others%20[IPAB%20order].pdf.
9. *Civil Appeal Nos. 2706-2716 of 2013* (decision of the Supreme Court of India, Civil Appellate Jurisdiction, arising out of SLP(C) Nos. 20539-20549 of 2009), http://judis.nic.in/supremecourt/imgs1.aspx?filename=40212.
10. "*Roche v. Cipla*: Final Leg of Battle over the Tarceva Patent" (RNA IP Attorneys, India, Feb. 2, 2016), http://www.lexology.com/library/detail.aspx?g=bc7dd620-6e3a-4888-a18a-21ada73cd544.

11. Maitri Porecha, "Piramal Move to Shut Mumbai R&D Affects Scientists," *DNA* (Mumbai, Sept. 3, 2014), http://www.dnaindia.com/money/report-piramal-move-to-shut-mumbai-rd-affects-scientists-2015792.
12. R. Joseph, "Pharmaceutical Industry and Public Policy in Post-reform India" (Routledge India, 2015): 95–96.
13. Yuji Watanabe, "Pharmaceutical Intellectual Property Protection in India" (report, TRIPS Study Group, Institute for International Trade and Investment, 2009), https://www.jpo.go.jp/cgi/link.cgi?url=/shiryou/toushin/chousa/trips_chousa_houkoku.htm.
14. Kamal Dua et al., "NDDS Scenario in India: Vital Role of Pharma Professionals," Pharmainfo.net (Aug. 14, 2007).
15. Pharmabiz.com, "NDDS: New Lease of Life to an Old Molecule" (Feb. 26, 2004).
16. FY2004 Asia Industrial Foundation Empowerment Program (study for deepening Japan-India relations by field, Japan Research Institute, Feb. 2005): 196.

Chapter 7
Applicability of Section 3 (d)

This chapter discusses the applicability of Section 3 (d). Besides India, there are several other developing and newly industrialized countries which have large-scale pharmaceutical industries. This chapter starts by considering whether or not India's Section 3 (d) could be applicable to patent laws in any of those countries.

Then, this chapter explores the possibility that Section 3 (d) could be applicable to another industry besides the pharmaceutical industry. There are several other industries which have experienced rapid development. Could Section 3 (d), which played a successful negative impact mitigation role for India's pharmaceutical industry, do the same for another industry?

7.1 An Analysis of Applicability of Section 3 (d) to Other Developing Countries

As mentioned above (Sect. 1.2.2 "TRIPS Enforcement and Background to Introduction of Product Patents"), when the TRIPS Agreement came into force, all members of TRIPS, including developing countries, were required to introduce product patents (Note: Some grace periods were granted to developing countries and those that did not have product patents as of 1995) [1].

Under the TRIPS framework, all member countries, including developing countries, are required to revise their patent laws and introduce product patents. That means that many developing countries are now required to introduce product patents.

The author firmly believes that this study will have significant implications for those developing countries as they attempt to determine the most suitable patent frameworks for their respective situations.

Y. Mitsumori, *The Indian Pharmaceutical Industry*,
SpringerBriefs in Health Care Management and Economics,
https://doi.org/10.1007/978-981-10-6790-7_7

In earlier chapters, this study discussed two factors that made it possible for insertion of Section 3 (d) into the Patents (Amendment) Act, 2005 to work successfully.

The first one was the transition of business models of the Indian pharmaceutical industry; the big players in the industry changed their business model from an exclusively generic drugs business one to an integrated business model embracing both generic drugs and brand-name drugs business. The second factor was the insertion of Section 3 (d) into the Patents (Amendment) Act, 2005.

However, not every country can change its pharmaceutical industry business model from an exclusively generics one to an integrated model.

In order to be able to make that transition, the country needs to have a high standard of pharmaceutical technology [2].

In order for a clause like Section 3 (d) to play an effective role in protecting a country's pharmaceutical industry, that industry needs to be of a certain scale.

The question, then, is which countries have the high levels of technology and the appropriate scale of pharmaceutical industry? Some African countries have introduced product patents over the past several years. However, there are no reports from these countries indicating that introduction of product patents had negative impacts on their pharmaceutical industries. That is because there were virtually no pharmaceutical industries in those countries.

The story in India was different. When product patents were introduced there in 2005, it became a big issue, not just in India but worldwide. There were several reasons:

1. By that time, the Indian pharmaceutical industry had become the fourth largest in the world (in terms of volume) [3].
2. Indian pharmaceutical products—which were actually "copies" of foreign-manufactured patented drugs produced in India utilizing reverse engineering technology—were selling well, not just in the Indian market but internationally [4].
3. The Indian pharmaceutical industry had attained a very high technological level [5].
4. Indian products accounted for up to 80% of the AIDS drugs supplied by International NPOs (such as MSF) to Third World countries where huge numbers of poor people were in need of treatment [6].

Therefore, the two factors mentioned above—(1) the country's pharmaceutical industry should have a high level of technology, and (2) the country's pharmaceutical industry should have a certain scale—need to be present in order for "insertion of Section 3 (d)" and "transition of the pharmaceutical industry's business model" to be effective in mitigating negative impacts resulting from introduction of product patents in the country concerned.

The question here is: Which countries can satisfy those two conditions?

According to Yamane, the World Bank in its 1986 report noted that "from a technological development point of view, it is difficult for developing countries to have effective pharmaceutical industries."

However, the report highlighted Korea and Turkey as "exceptional countries" [7].

Fifteen years later, in 2010, IMS Health released a new report titled "Pharmerging Shake-Up: New Imperatives in a Redefined World." In the report, IMS Health designated 17 countries as "pharmerging markets" and projected that the combined value of those countries' pharmaceutical markets would expand by US$90 billion between 2009 and 2013, accounting for 48% of annual pharmaceutical market growth [8].

The report classified the 17 countries into three tiers. Tier 1 included only China, which, according to the report, was expected to become the world's third-largest pharmaceutical manufacturing country by 2011, with growth of US$40+ billion projected through 2013.

The second tier included Brazil, India, and Russia, which were expected to add between US$5 billion and US$15 billion in annual sales by 2013.

The third-tier countries included Venezuela, Poland, Argentina, Turkey, Mexico, Vietnam, South Africa, Thailand, Indonesia, Romania, Egypt, Pakistan, and Ukraine. These 13 countries were each expected to contribute between US$1 billion and US$5 billion in annual sales growth by 2013 [8].

As mentioned above, for Section 3 (d) to be able to play a mitigation role, the country needs to satisfy two conditions:

1. Its pharmaceutical industry must have a high level of technology.
2. The industry must be of a certain scale.

Almost all of the 17 "pharmerging markets" designated by IMS Health can meet the second condition in that they have pharmaceutical industries of a certain scale. However, only a few can satisfy the first condition—having a pharmaceutical industry with a high level of technology [9].

Will these countries adopt Section 3 (d) or a similar type of clause in their patent laws? Moreover, if such a clause were to be inserted into their patent laws, would it produce the same impact mitigation effect that was experienced in India?

It is said that Section 3 (d) is unique to Indian patent law. As of 2005, India was the only country to have such a clause.

The Economic Times, an Indian daily, reported on August 13, 2007, that the "Maldives, Pakistan, Sri Lanka, Vietnam, Indonesia, Malaysia and Bangladesh are actively considering adopting Section 3 (d) of the Indian patent law" [10].

As reported in *The Economic Times*, several developing countries and newly industrialized countries were considering introducing Section 3 (d) or a similar type of clause to safeguard their pharmaceutical industries against foreign-owned companies; however, to date, only a few countries have a Section 3 (d) or similar clause in their patent laws. (Note: There was a report that the Philippines had introduced a Section 3 (d) type clause into its patent law.)

This study features Brazil, which boasts the world's sixth-largest pharmaceutical market and has a special system of linkage between patent approval and market approval.

7.1.1 *Brazilian Safeguard Framework: Patent Linkage and Compulsory Licensing*

As of 2012, the Brazilian Pharmaceutical Market was worth US$24.8 billion and ranked No. 6 in the world [11].

Brazil had product patent protection until 1945. However, the country revised its patent law in 1945 and abolished product patents in the pharmaceutical, food, and agricultural chemical fields.

In 1969, even process patents on pharmaceuticals were abolished, allowing Brazilian pharmaceutical companies to "copy" drugs whose patents were protected outside of Brazil without infringing local patent laws [12].

This arrangement was supposed to give advantages to the Brazilian pharmaceutical industry and to disadvantage foreign-owned companies. However, despite being given such a helping hand, the Brazilian pharmaceutical industry failed to develop, and it was outperformed by foreign-owned companies in both the API/bulk and formulations markets [13].

Brazil had assumed the role of leader of the developing countries in a series of TRIPS conferences, always taking an opposing position against the advanced countries group led by the US. It maintained that stance even after the TRIPS Agreement came into force in 1995. Nevertheless, in 1996, one year after TRIPS enforcement, Brazil revised its patent law to make it TRIPS compliant [14].

However, Brazil has been restricting patent enforcement within the country through use of two measures: patent linkage and compulsory licensing.

1. Patent Linkage

As mentioned above, Brazil revised its patent law in 1996 and introduced product patents. The Brazilian Industrial Property Law (Brazilian Patent Law) does not contain any Section 3 (d) or similar clause.

Instead, the country has made it difficult for applicants to obtain patent approval in the pharmaceutical field by linking patent approval and marketing approval [15].

Specifically, according to the Brazilian Industrial Property Law (Brazilian Patent Law) 229C, an applicant for a patent in the pharmaceutical field is required to obtain consent for the molecule from ANVISA (the Brazilian Health Regulatory Agency) prior to filing a patent application [16].

Article 229 C of the Brazilian Industrial Property Law (Brazilian Patent Law) stipulates:

The grant of patents for pharmaceutical products and processes shall depend upon the prior approval from the National Sanitary Vigilance Agency (ANVISA) [17].

In other words, the article provides that patents for pharmaceutical products and processes might only be granted after the applicant has received prior consent from the Brazilian equivalent of the US FDA. Section 229-C was introduced into Brazilian Patent Law by Law No. 10.196 of February 14, 2001.

ANVISA, established in 1999, is a government agency which is responsible for determining if products or services could potentially be harmful to public health, and for granting marketing approval for certain types of products, including pharmaceuticals.

Several cases have been reported in which the Brazilian Patent Office, based on three criteria—novelty, industrial applicability, and inventive steps—decided to grant patents for goods or services in the pharmaceutical field; however, ANVISA declined to give approval for the subjects of those applications [15].

As noted earlier (Sect. 2.2 "Remarkable Features of the Pharmaceutical Industry from the Perspective of Patent Protection"), pharmaceutical companies tend to submit their patent applications during the early drug discovery stage. But, typically, they do not submit new drug applications (NDAs) until after all clinical trials have been completed and all of the necessary data are compiled. Naturally, there are very long time gaps between patent application and NDA submission.

If patent application and NDA submission are linked, pharmaceutical companies cannot submit patent applications in the early stages; instead, they are required to submit patent applications at the end of clinical trials stage. Such an arrangement can delay pharmaceutical patent approval.

Yamane, in her book, noted that there have been several cases where, even though the Brazilian Patent Office admitted patentability of goods or services, ANVISA did not give approval [18].

2. Compulsory Licensing

Article 31 of the TRIPS Agreement allows compulsory licensing and government use of a patent without authorization by its owner.

However, the article stipulates that a compulsory license should only be issued under conditions such as the following: (1) a person who plans to apply for a compulsory license must first attempt to obtain a voluntary license from the IP holder; and (2) the applicant shall pay adequate remuneration to the IP holder.

Even if the applicant is granted a compulsory license, exporting of the product or service concerned to a third country is prohibited [19].

However, at the 4th WTO Ministerial Meeting in Doha on November 14, 2001, a Declaration on the TRIPS agreement and public health was adopted [20].

Under the declaration, WTO member countries were permitted to issue compulsory licenses in order to protect public health.

There was a further step. The WTO General Council on August 30, 2003, adopted "Implementation of paragraph 6 of the Doha Declaration on the TRIPS Agreement and public health." Under the declaration, least-developed countries which have insufficient or no manufacturing capacity in the pharmaceutical sector are allowed to import pharmaceutical products produced by an exporting country which has granted or intends to grant a compulsory license in accordance with Article 31 of the TRIPS Agreement [21].

The Brazilian government in 2007 issued a compulsory license for the AIDS drug efavirenz after price negotiations with Merck (the IP holder for efavirenz) had broken down [22].

As mentioned above, the TRIPS Agreement allows member countries to issue compulsory licenses under certain conditions. Utilizing the scheme, other countries besides Brazil have also issued compulsory licenses.

Thailand issued three compulsory licenses between 2006 and 2007 for Sustiva (efavirenz), an anti-HIV drug by Merck; Kaletra (lopinavir/ritonavir), an anti-HIV drug by Abbott; and Plavix (clopidogrel), a heart attack or stroke drug by Bristol-Myers Squibb. The compulsory license for Plavix generated considerable international debate because, thus far, compulsory licenses had only been issued for AIDS-HIV drugs; however, Thailand, for the first time, had issued a compulsory license for a drug for chronic conditions such as heart attack and stroke [23].

Yamane pointed out that developing countries, including Brazil, have used compulsory licensing for the purposes of price negotiation rather than for attempting to enable a local pharmaceutical company to produce a patented drug [24].

3. Applicability of Section 3 (d) to the Brazilian Industry

As mentioned above, Brazil has been utilizing two measures—(a) patent linkage and (b) compulsory licensing—to protect the Brazilian pharmaceutical industry against foreign-owned companies.

According to EMIS, the Brazilian pharmaceutical market was worth US$24.8 billion as of 2012 and ranked No. 6 in the world. Brazil has a large pharmaceutical market [11].

As mentioned above, IMS Health in 2010 selected Brazil as one of 17 "pharmerging markets," placing the Brazilian market on Tier 2, and predicted that it would grow rapidly, going forward [8].

Brazil appears to meet one of the two conditions for Section 3 (d) applicability—it has a pharmaceutical industry of a certain scale. However, Brazil's technology level is not as high as that of India [25].

Taking these factors into consideration, it would seem to be impossible for Brazil to enjoy mitigation of negative impacts of introduction of product patents, even if the Brazilian government were to insert Section 3 (d) or a similar clause into its patent law.

However, as IMS Health reported, the pharmaceutical markets of newly developing countries have been expanding rapidly. As those markets develop, their technology levels could improve. In fact, Brazil at one time attempted to develop pharmaceutical research and development technology and poured a great deal of money into the effort. If such efforts could produce certain outcomes and the technology level improved, the country might be able to obtain the mitigation effect as a result of inserting a Section 3 (d) type clause in its patent law.

7.2 Applicability of Section 3 (d) to Other Industries

Through the analysis in Chap. 5—analysis of various data—and that in Chap. 6—a series of interviews with stakeholders—this study has shown that Section 3 (d) served to protect the Indian pharmaceutical industry against foreign-owned companies and allowed the industry to keep growing, as was intended by the Indian government.

In order for Section 3 (d) to play a role in protecting a country's pharmaceutical industry, the industry needs to be of a certain scale.

The next question is whether or not Section 3 (d) is applicable to industries other than the pharmaceutical industry.

Could Section 3 (d) have a negative impact mitigation effect in respect of other industries?

As mentioned above, (Sect. 2.2 Remarkable Features of the Pharmaceutical Industry from the Perspective of Patent Protection), impacts of patents differ from one industry to another. As discussed in Sect. 2.2, in the IT industry, companies quite often deal their IPs between them (in so-called cross-licensing practice) in order to develop new products in a relatively short time.

It is impossible for Section 3 (d) to provide negative impact mitigation effects in industries in which a number of IPs are cross-licensed to facilitate new product development.

Insertion of Section 3 (d) into the Indian Patents (Amendment) Act, 2005 had various effects: (1) It provided protection to the domestic market for a certain period; (2) during that period, the industry developed new technology and new products which had potential for further development; and (3) local consumers were more motivated to purchase products developed in their own country by domestic manufacturers.

Section 3 (d) had negative impact mitigation effects in those segments where (1) the number of patents required to develop a new product is quite small; (2) it takes a long time to develop a new product.

The IT industry is strikingly different from the pharmaceutical industry in both respects. No one would expect Section 3 (d) to have the same effects in the IT industry as it did in the Indian pharmaceutical industry.

The question that arises here is: In which industries might Section 3 (d) have negative impact mitigation effects? Biotechnology could be one candidate.

Biotechnology is a relatively new industrial field for India. Until recently, the market was quite small. However, the biotechnology field has been experiencing rapid development.

According to IBEF "Biotechnology" (August 2015), the biotechnology market in India was only worth US$1.1 billion in FY2005. Since then, the market has developed rapidly, reaching US$7 billion in FY2015 [26] (Fig. 7.1).

The Indian biotechnology industry is divided into five segments:

(a) Biopharmaceuticals are therapeutic or preventative drugs derived from materials that are naturally present in living organisms, such as vaccines, insulin, monoclonal antibodies, EPO, and interferon.
(b) Bio-services include clinical research and CRO as well as custom manufacturing.
(c) Bio-agriculture is segmented into hybrid seeds, transgenic crops, biopesticides, and bio-fertilizers.
(d) Bio-industrial comprises enzyme manufacturing and marketing companies.
(e) Bioinformatics companies provide services for the creation and maintenance of extensive electronic databases on various biological systems [27].

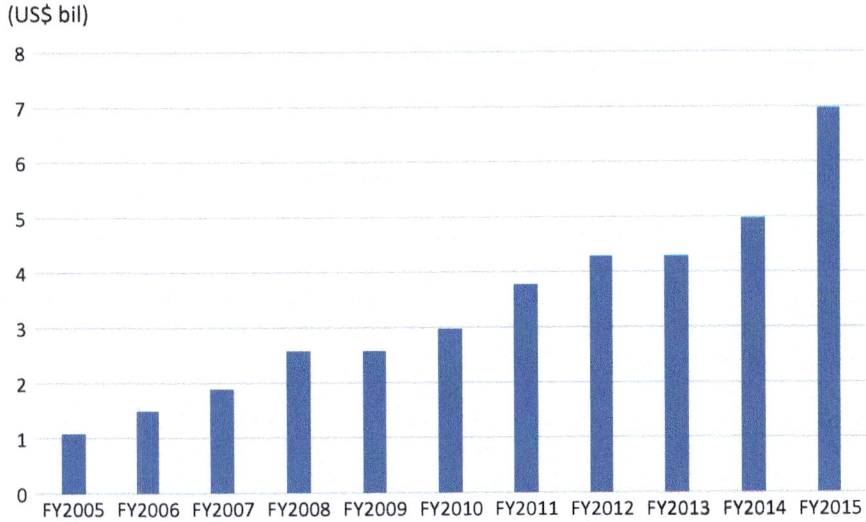

Fig. 7.1 Indian biotechnology market growth (FY05–FY15) (*Source*: IBEF, Ref. [26])

Fig. 7.2 Market share of each biotechnology segment (*Source*: IBEF, Ref. [27])

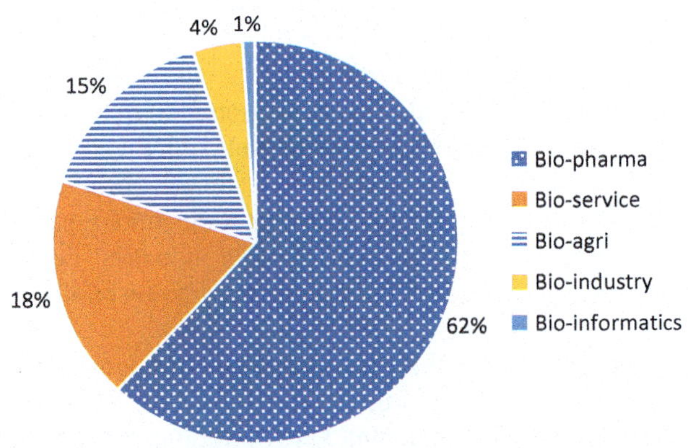

Shares of each of these five segments are shown in Fig. 7.2.

IBEF estimates that the Indian biotechnology market will grow to US$100 billion by FY2025. To support healthy development of the industry, the Indian government announced that it would allocate a total US$3.7 billion to biotechnology in India's 12th Five Year Plan (2012–2017).

As the biotechnology market grows and R&D investment in this field rises, the number of products and services available increases and so does the number of patent applications in the biotechnology field.

Figure 7.3 shows the recent trend of patent applications in the biotechnology field in India [28].

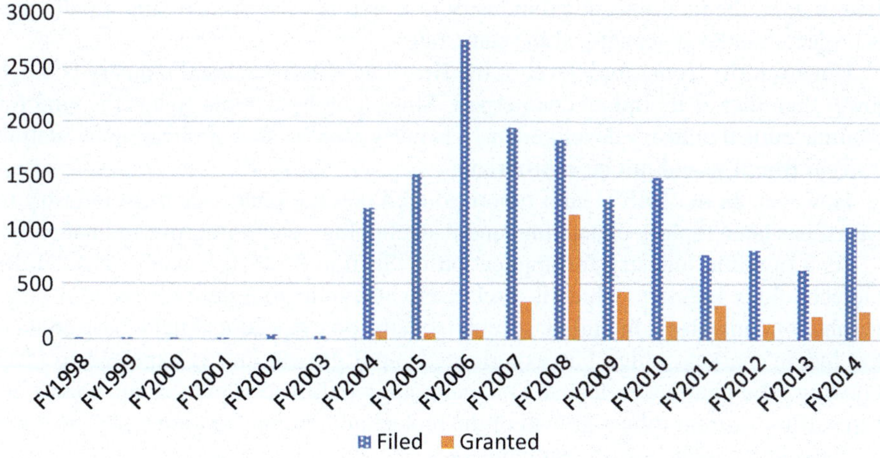

Fig. 7.3 Biotechnology-related patent applications (1998–2014) (*Source*: IPO Annual Report (There was no data for granted between FY1998 and FY2003))

A number of foreign-owned companies have invested in India's biotechnology markets. Major investors include Tekes (Finland), Sanofi Aventis (France), and Mylan, Abbott Laboratories, and GE Healthcare (US). Meanwhile, there are a handful of very strong Indian companies in this field: Biocon, Serum Institute of India, and Panacea Biotech [29].

As mentioned, the biotechnology market consists of five segments: biopharmaceuticals, bio-services, bio-agriculture, bio-industrial, and bioinformatics. In fact, the pharmaceutical market and the biotechnology market overlap to some extent.

The biotechnology and pharmaceutical markets have similar characteristics: (a) one patent plays a very important role in development of a new product; (b) it takes longer to develop a new product; and (c) the pharmaceutical market and some parts of the biotechnology market are regulated. A company needs to obtain approval in order to do business.

Because these two markets have similar characteristics, if a Section 3 (d) type clause were introduced in the biotechnology field, the clause might have played a similar role to that of Section 3 (d) in the pharmaceutical market—protecting Indian companies against foreign-owned companies.

7.3 Possibilities for Section 3 (d)

This chapter examined possible applicability of Section 3 (d) in another developing or newly developing country and in another industry.

As a possible country in which Section 3 (d) might be applied, this study selected Brazil whose pharmaceutical market ranks No. 6 in the world. As shown by IMS

Health data, the pharmaceutical industry in Brazil has been expanding rapidly and is projected to keep growing at the same rate.

However, the technology level of the Brazilian pharmaceutical industry is much lower than that of its Indian counterpart. Since a high-technology level is vital for pharmaceutical industry development, it is fairly obvious that application of Section 3 (d) in Brazil would not be appropriate.

However, as the IMS Health report pointed out, the pharmaceutical industry in Brazil has been rapidly expanding, and its technology could improve dramatically.

As a possible industry for application of Section 3 (d), this study selected the biotechnology industry, which is a relatively new industrial field for India. A large number of companies, including several from the pharmaceutical field, have entered the Indian market, which has experienced rapid growth and is expected to keep growing. The pharmaceutical and biotechnology industries share certain characteristics. If the current robust growth of the biotechnology industry continues, Section 3 (d) could be applicable in that industry.

References

1. Keiji Iwata, "The Effect of the Indian Patent Law Amendment," *Patent* 61, no. 2 (Feb. 2008): 42.
2. Hiroko Yamane, *Interpreting TRIPS: Globalisation of Intellectual Property Rights and Access to Medicines* (Iwanami Shoten, 2008), 4.
3. Tata Strategic Management Group, "Asia Business Generator Project: Overview of the Indian Pharmaceutical Industry" (March 2008): 1.
4. Yaeko Mitsumori, "Study on the Roles of the Section 3d of the Indian Patent Act for Lightening Negative Impact of Product Patent Introduction in 2005 on Indian Pharmaceutical Industry," *The Journal of Japan MOT Society, Japan MOT Society, Technology and Economics*, no. 526 (Dec. 2010): 51.
5. "The Current Status of the Indian Pharmaceutical Industry" (research materials, no. 400, The Japan Pharmaceutical Manufacturers Association [JPMA], July 2009): 6.
6. MSF Website, "Why India's Generic Medicines Industry Is So Important," http://www.doctorswithoutborders.org/news-stories/field-news/why-indias-generic-medicines-industry-so-important.
7. Hiroko Yamane, *Interpreting TRIPS: Globalisation of Intellectual Property Rights and Access to Medicines* (Iwanami Shoten, 2008), 183.
8. IMS World Review Executive, "Pharmerging Shake-Up: New Imperatives in a Redefined World" (IMS press release, March 16, 2010).
9. Hiroko Yamane, *Interpreting TRIPS: Globalisation of Intellectual Property Rights and Access to Medicines* (Iwanami Shoten, 2008), 171-172.
10. G. Prasad, "Copycats Popping Patent Law Pill," *The Economic Times*, Aug. 13, 2007, http://articles.economictimes.indiatimes.com/2007-08-13/news/27677651_1_patent-law-section-3d-dg-shah.
11. "Pharmaceutical Sector Brazil" (EMIS, Euromoney Institutional Investor Company, Dec. 2013): 4.
12. Rafael Brandão, "Brazilian Patent System: A Brief Introduction" (National Institute of Industrial Property, Brazil, January 2012): 4.
13. Hiroko Yamane, *Interpreting TRIPS: Globalisation of Intellectual Property Rights and Access to Medicines* (Iwanami Shoten, 2008), 173.

14. Hiroko Yamane, *Interpreting TRIPS: Globalisation of Intellectual Property Rights and Access to Medicines* (Iwanami Shoten, 2008), 139.
15. "Ch. 4: An Analysis of TRIPS Compatibility of the Brazilian Industrial Property Law, International IP System Study Group 2012" (report compiled by Mitsubishi UFJ Research and Consulting, March 2012): 16-19, http://www.jpo.go.jp/shiryou/toushin/chousa/pdf/tripschousahoukoku/23_4.pdf.
16. Eduardo Da Gama Camara Jr., "Prosecution of Pharmaceutical Patents in Brazil: Tensions between the Brazilian Patent Office and ANVISA," *Mondaq* (July 22, 2013).
17. WIPO Website, "Brazilian Industrial Property Law," http://www.wipo.int/wipolex/en/details.jsp?id=515.
18. Hiroko Yamane, *Interpreting TRIPS: Globalisation of Intellectual Property Rights and Access to Medicines* (Iwanami Shoten, 2008), 182.
19. WTO Website, "Does the Agreement Allow Compulsory Licensing of Patents?" (Frequently Asked Questions about TRIPS in the WTO), https://www.wto.org/english/tratop_e/trips_e/tripfq_e.htm.
20. WTO Website, "Doha WTO Ministerial 2001: TRIPS Declaration on the TRIPS Agreement and Public Health" (adopted on Nov. 14, 2001), https://www.wto.org/english/thewto_e/minist_e/min01_e/mindecl_trips_e.htm.
21. "Implementation of Paragraph 6 of the Doha Declaration on the TRIPS Agreement and Public Health," https://www.wto.org/english/tratop_e/TRIPs_e/implem_para6_e.htm.
22. E. Bond and K. Saggi, K., "Compulsory Licensing, Price Controls, and Access to Patented Foreign Products" (paper, Vanderbilt University, April 2012), http://www.wipo.int/edocs/mdocs/mdocs/en/wipo_ip_econ_ge_4_12/wipo_ip_econ_ge_4_12_ref_saggi.pdf.
23. Program on Information Justice and Intellectual Property Website, "Timeline for US-Thailand Compulsory License Dispute Version 3," (April 2009), http://infojustice.org/wp-content/uploads/2012/11/pijip-thailand-timeline.pdf.
24. Hiroko Yamane, *Interpreting TRIPS: Globalisation of Intellectual Property Rights and Access to Medicines* (Iwanami Shoten, 2008), 183.
25. Hiroko Yamane, *Interpreting TRIPS: Globalisation of Intellectual Property Rights and Access to Medicines* (Iwanami Shoten, 2008), 173.
26. IBEF, "Biotechnology" (Aug. 2015): 10.
27. IBEF, "Biotechnology" (Aug. 2015): 11.
28. IPO Annual Report (1998-2014).
29. Make in India Biotechnology Website, http://www.makeinindia.com/sector/biotechnology.

Chapter 8
Conclusions and Future Challenges

The insertion of Section 3 (d) into the Patents (Amendment) Act, 2005 of India stands as one successful model for developing and newly industrialized countries that need to introduce product patents in order to comply with WTO and TRIPS requirements.

However, the Indian model will not work in all developing and newly industrialized countries. In order for this Indian model to work effectively, the country concerned should have a high level of pharmaceutical technology and a pharmaceutical market of a certain scale. This chapter reviews the material presented in Chaps. 1, 2, 3, 4, 5, 6, and 7 and examines future challenges.

8.1 Review of Chapters

Chapter 1 started by establishing the background to this study. It showed why the author of this study chose design of patent law in a developing country as the research subject and the reason for selection of India, where product patents were introduced after the country's pharmaceutical industry grew to rank No. 4 in the world, as a case study for examining the impacts of patent law revision on industries.

Section 1.2 of Chap. 1 outlined the current status of the Indian pharmaceutical industry and Indian government policy on patent protection.

It explained that India was required to introduce product patents due to enforcement of the TRIPS Agreement and that, taking advantage of the TRIPS requirements, the Indian pharmaceutical industry changed its business model from an exclusively generic drugs business model based on reverse engineering technology to an integrated business model embracing both generic drugs and brand-name drugs.

Y. Mitsumori, *The Indian Pharmaceutical Industry*,
SpringerBriefs in Health Care Management and Economics,
https://doi.org/10.1007/978-981-10-6790-7_8

The section also described how a heated debate regarding the impacts of introduction of product patents into India erupted, not just in India but worldwide.

It posed two research questions based on the discussion: First, "whether or not insertion of Section 3 (d) into the Patents (Amendment) Act, 2005 protected the Indian pharmaceutical industry against foreign-owned companies as the Indian government intended" and, second, "if the Indian pharmaceutical industry was able to achieve robust development, mitigating the negative impacts of introduction of product patents, because their change of business model worked successfully."

Section 3 described the objectives and implications of this study.

The objective is to clarify whether or not insertion of Section 3 (d) into the Patents (Amendment) Act, 2005 mitigated negative impacts of introduction of product patents, as is suggested in prior literature. The discussion in this study is intended to have significant implications for other developing countries which need to introduce product patents at some point as they work to formulate patent regimes that are appropriate for their respective situations.

Chapter 2 described the Indian pharmaceutical industry and the transition of Indian patent law.

Currently, the Indian pharmaceutical industry accounts for only 2.4% of the global pharmaceutical market; however, it has been growing rapidly.

The industry maintains a very high level of technology. Indian pharmaceutical companies are marketing branded generics. Although drugs for acute conditions have a large share of the Indian pharmaceutical market, the share of chronic disease drugs, such as lifestyle disease drugs, has been increasing rapidly.

The chapter also explained how inclusion of Section 3 (d) in the Patents (Amendment) Act, 2005 restricts patentability of goods and services.

Chapter 3 showed research subjects and analytical methods. The chapter first demonstrated the hypothesis of this study, "Section 3 (d), inserted into the Patents (Amendment) Act, 2005 by the Indian government, served to mitigate the negative impact that introduction of product patents would normally have on a country's economy," and outlined the research framework.

Chapter 4 analyzed prior literature. Once it was decided under the TRIPS Agreement that all developing countries would be required to introduce product patents, considerable debate around the issue ensued. As a result, a number of studies were conducted and numerous papers were presented.

This study analyzed relevant literature, reports, and commissioned papers across four categories: (a) developing countries and patent law; (b) impact of introduction of product patents; (c) Section 3 (d) of the Patents (Amendment) Act, 2005; and (d) transition of business model of Indian pharmaceutical industry.

The prior literature analysis showed that, when product patents are introduced into developing countries, including India, welfare losses are generated. However, large Indian pharmaceutical companies boosted R&D investment and initiated NCE development, taking advantage of TRIPS enforcement and the introduction of product patents.

It was also found that Section 3 (d) contains some problems, such as vague expressions.

Chapter 5 analyzed indicators for the Indian pharmaceutical industry.

Section 5.1 of Chap. 5 explained the analytical methods, and subsequent sections showed the results of analyses utilizing six indicators—stock prices analysis, business performance analysis (sales and profits), R&D investment analysis, new drug development pipeline analysis, patent application analysis, and trade activities analysis (exports and imports of pharmaceutical products).

The section also analyzed the transition of business models based on various secondary data. Using data on R&D structures and business organizational changes collected from a variety of sources, including annual reports of major Indian pharmaceutical companies and Indian media reports, the chapter analyzed relationships with the transition of the business models of Indian companies.

From analysis of annual reports, this study found that major Indian pharmaceutical companies decided to transition their organizations into innovation-based businesses, changed their business models, and initiated NCE development.

An analysis of research structures found that several major Indian pharmaceutical companies had set up their own research centers and initiated new drug development programs.

A local paper reported that a large number of pharmaceutical research centers had been built in India "because, after a new patent protection law was enacted, Indian companies could no longer ignore the patents of multinational drug companies and produce unlicensed generics."

An analysis of company organizations found that several major Indian pharmaceutical companies set up subsidiary companies designed to specialize in new drug development, partly as a way to insulate parent companies against the high risks associated with new drug development.

Chapter 6 analyzed a series of interviews with various stakeholders in India, which were conducted to complement the data analysis in Chap. 5. This chapter also analyzed cases related to Section 3 (d); one was a patent application rejection case; the other was a patent infringement lawsuit.

Section 6.1 of Chap. 6 provided outlines of the interviews conducted with various stakeholders in India for the purpose of examining if insertion of Section 3 (d) into the Patents (Amendment) Act, 2005 served to mitigate the negative impacts of introduction of product patents.

Section 2 explained the results of those interviews.

An interview with IDMA, an association for small- to medium-sized Indian pharmaceutical companies, revealed that (1) Section 3 (d) was drafted jointly by IDMA and the Indian government; in other words, the Indian government inserted Section 3 (d) into the Patents (Amendment) Act, 2005 with the intention of protecting the Indian pharmaceutical industry against foreign-owned companies; and (2) the role of Section 3 (d) was to protect the Indian pharmaceutical industry, not to enable the granting of patents for trivial improvements.

An interview with OPPI, an association of foreign-owned pharmaceutical companies, revealed that those companies were concerned about Section 3 (d) and hoped for its abolition.

Section 6.4 of Chap. 6 analyzed two cases related to Section 3 (d).

First was the Indian Patent Office's rejection of Novartis' Gleevec patent application and the ensuing court case. This was one example of a number of cases where the Indian Patent Office had rejected patent applications for internationally patented drugs on the basis of Section 3 (d).

Second was a series of court battles between Roche and Cipla regarding Tarceva (erlotinib). This was an example of at least one Indian pharmaceutical company initiating production of a patented drug without permission from the IP holder, on the basis of Section 3 (d), and an Indian court (Delhi High Court) permitting production to continue until at least the date of final judgment.

Chapter 7 discussed the roles of Section 3 (d) of the Patents (Amendment) Act, 2005.

Section 7.1 of Chap. 7 discussed possible applicability of Section 3 (d) to Brazil, the world's sixth-largest pharmaceutical market. The section described how Brazil restricts the scope of patents utilizing two safeguarding frameworks: patent linkage and compulsory licensing. Although Brazil has a large-scale pharmaceutical market, the technology level of the Brazilian pharmaceutical industry is not as high as that of India. On that basis, this study concluded that, even if Section 3 (d) or a similar clause were to be inserted into Brazilian patent law, the Brazilian pharmaceutical industry would not be able to obtain the same negative impact mitigation effects.

Section 7.2 of Chap. 7 discussed possible applicability of Section 3 (d) to another industry. Earlier, in Sect. 2.2, this study explained the difference between the role played by IP in the IT industry and that in the pharmaceutical industry. Section 7.2 of Chap. 7 reiterated the differences between the IT industry and the pharmaceutical industry and noted that it would be difficult to apply Section 3 (d) to the IT industry, which has very different characteristics from the pharmaceutical industry.

This section then selected the biotechnology industry as a possible candidate for Section 3 (d) application.

It showed that the biotechnology market and the pharmaceutical market share several similar characteristics, such as (a) one patent plays a very important role in development of a new product; (b) it takes longer to develop a new product; and (c) the pharmaceutical market and some parts of the biotechnology market are regulated.

Based on these analyses, this section concluded that, if Section 3 (d) were to be applied in respect of the biotechnology field, it could play some kind of safeguarding role to help protect Indian companies against foreign-owned companies. However, the section also noted that some areas of the biotechnology industry overlap with parts of the pharmaceutical industry.

8.2 Conclusion

This study examined reasons why the Indian pharmaceutical industry continued on a growth trajectory even after introduction of product patents in 2005, without being affected by negative impacts of such introduction.

Through a two-step analysis in Chaps. 5 and 6, it was revealed that (a) the Indian pharmaceutical industry's self-help efforts—changing its business model from a conventional purely generic drugs business model to an integrated one embracing both generics and brand-name drugs—and (b) Indian government policy in the form of insertion of Section 3 (d) into the Patents (Amendment) Act, 2005 produced a synergistic effect and allowed the Indian pharmaceutical industry to keep developing.

Through that two-step analysis, the working hypothesis set up in Chap. 4: "Indian government effort—inserting the safeguarding clause Section 3 (d) into the Patents (Amendment) Act, 2005—and the Indian pharmaceutical industry's self-help efforts—changing its business model from a conventional purely generics business model to an integrated business model; embracing both generic drugs (off-patent drugs) and brand-name drugs (patented drugs)—created a synergistic effect which eventually mitigated the negative impact that a developing country would normally sustain in the wake of introduction of product patents"—was proved.

Accordingly, this study's main hypothesis—"Insertion of Section 3 (d) into the Patents (Amendment) Act, 2005 by the Indian government played a role of mitigating the negative impacts which introduction of product patents would normally impose on a country's economy"—was proved.

TRIPS, enforced in 1995, requires all member countries, including developing countries, to introduce product patents. India has successfully fulfilled its TRIPS commitment by introducing "a TRIPS-compatible law" while also protecting its domestic industry against foreign-owned companies through insertion of a unique clause, Section 3 (d), into its patent law.

This Indian example stands as a successful model for other developing countries which are required to introduce product patents. In particular, the example of role-sharing between the industry and the government could show the way for other developing countries as they work to formulate effective industrial frameworks.

However, as this study discussed in Chap. 7, this Indian model would not be applicable to all developing countries. In order for a country's pharmaceutical industry to change its business model into an integrated business model embracing both generic drugs and brand-name drugs, the country needs to have a high level of pharmaceutical technology. Moreover, in order for Section 3 (d) type clause to play an effective role in protecting the country's pharmaceutical industry, that industry needs to be of a certain scale. If the country can pass those two tests, the Indian model might be applicable.

This study analyzed possible applicability to Brazil, which has a huge pharmaceutical market. However, the technology level is not very high. It appears that

Brazilian pharmaceutical companies have not been engaging in any new drug development and there are no molecules in their pipelines. Even if the Indian model were to be applied in Brazil, it does not seem likely that Brazil would obtain the negative impact mitigation effects.

However, as IMS Health and some other market watchers have reported, pharmaceutical industries and markets in developing and newly industrialized countries have been developing very rapidly.

Some developing and newly industrialized countries may catch up to India and gain highly advanced pharmaceutical technology in the near future. If that happens, the Indian model might then be applicable to those countries. Section 3 (d) or a similar clause could mitigate negative impacts of the introduction of product patents in such markets.

As a possible applicable field for the Indian model, this study examined the biotechnology industry. The biotechnology industry has been on a steep development trajectory. In India, domestic companies hold large market shares, and they have been aggressively developing new products. In the biotechnology field, a single patent plays a significant role, and it takes a long time to develop a new product. If Section 3 (d) or a similar clause is adopted in the biotechnology field, it could help to protect the domestic industry against foreign-owned companies and provide a "soft landing" for local manufacturers.

8.3 Future Challenges

Since product patents were only introduced in India on January 1, 2005, it may be some time before the effects are fully reflected in the performance of the Indian pharmaceutical industry. Going forward, the market trend should be carefully monitored.

The Economic Times, an Indian daily, on August 13, 2007, reported that the "Maldives, Pakistan, Sri Lanka, Vietnam, Indonesia, Malaysia and Bangladesh are actively considering adopting Section 3 (d) of the Indian patent law" in their own patent laws.

Later, the paper also reported that the Philippines had revised its patent law and inserted a Section 3 (d) type clause into its patent law. Through comparing the roles of Section 3 (d) or a Section 3 (d)-like clause in other countries' patent laws, far deeper knowledge regarding Section 3 (d) might be obtained.

As noted in prior literature, insertion of Section 3 (d) into the Patents (Amendment) Act, 2005 was not without problems. For instance, the clause contains some vague expressions; it is unclear what "efficacy" means in this context or what degree of enhancement is deemed to be "significant enhancement." In order to examine the various issues inherent in Section 3 (d), it is useful to study similar clauses contained or to be included in other countries' patent laws.

Notes

Note 1: TRIPS
The WTO's Agreement on Trade-Related Aspects of Intellectual Property Rights (TRIPS), negotiated in the 1986–94 Uruguay Round, introduced intellectual property rules into the multilateral trading system for the first time.

The TRIPS Agreement is an attempt to narrow the gaps in the ways in which intellectual property (IP) rights are protected around the world and to bring them under common international rules. It establishes minimum levels of protection that each government has to give to the intellectual property of fellow WTO members. In doing so, it strikes a balance between the long-term benefits and possible short-term costs to society. Society benefits in the long term when intellectual property protection encourages creation and invention, especially when the period of protection expires and the creations and inventions enter the public domain. Governments are allowed to reduce any short-term costs through various exceptions; for example, to tackle public health problems. The Agreement sets out the minimum standards of intellectual property protection to be provided by each member.

Source: WTO Website, https://www.wto.org/english/thewto_e/whatis_e/tif_e/agrm7_e.htm.

Note 2: Minimum Standards
The TRIPS Agreement is a minimum standards agreement, which allows members to provide more extensive protection of intellectual property if they so wish. Members are left free to determine the appropriate method of implementing the provisions of the Agreement within their own legal system and practice.

Source: WTO Website, https://www.wto.org/english/tratop_e/trips_e/intel2_e.htm.

Note 3: Importance of Patents for the Pharmaceutical Industry
Patent protection for chemical and pharmaceutical products is especially important compared with other industries because the actual manufacturing process is often

Y. Mitsumori, *The Indian Pharmaceutical Industry*,
SpringerBriefs in Health Care Management and Economics,
https://doi.org/10.1007/978-981-10-6790-7

easy to replicate and can be copied with a fraction of the investment required for the research and clinical testing.

Source: Bruce Lehman, "The Pharmaceutical Industry and the Patent System," http://users.wfu.edu/mcfallta/DIR0/pharma_patents.pdf.

Note 4: Exemption of Product Patent in the Patents Act, 1970

The Patents Act, 1970 exempted product patents in the areas of pharmaceuticals, foods, and agricultural chemicals. In those three areas, process patent protection was maintained.

Source: WIPO Website, www.wipo.int/edocs/lexdocs/laws/en/in/in065en.pdf.

Note 5: Protectionist Policies Introduced by the Government of Indira Gandhi

Besides the patent law, other laws introduced in the 1970s also helped shape the protectionist stance of the Indian government. Specifically, in the early 1970s, the Monopolies and Restrictive Trade Practices Act, 1969 and the Foreign Exchange Regulation Act, 1973 were promulgated. These Acts were aimed at reducing the concentration of economic power by reducing foreign equity and controlling exports of foreign exchange. Indeed, the number of companies with a share of over 74% fell from 20 in 1976–1977 to 5 in 1981–1982.

Source: *Intellectual Property in Asia: Law, Economics, History and Politics*, ed. Paul Goldstein and Joseph Straus (Springer-Verlag Berlin Heidelberg, 2009)

Note 6: Background of the Patents Act, 1970

The Patents Act, 1970, along with the Patents Rules 1972, came into force on April 20, 1972, replacing the Indian Patents and Designs Act, 1911. The Patents Act was largely based on the recommendations of the Ayyangar Committee Report headed by Justice N. Rajagopala Ayyangar. One of the recommendations was the allowance of only process patents with regard to inventions relating to drugs, medicines, foods, and chemicals.

Source: Mondaq Website, http://www.mondaq.com/india/x/54494/Patent/Patent+Law+in+India.

Note 7: Indian Drug Manufacturers' Association (IDMA)

The Indian Drug Manufacturers' Association (IDMA), formed in 1961, works for Indian drug manufacturers' interests apart from protecting the interests of Indian consumers. It takes up policy issues related to implementation of the Drugs and Cosmetics Rules with central- or state-level authorities. It has a membership of over 900 Indian pharmaceutical companies. It issues a number of publications, including IDMA Bulletin; Indian Drugs; IDMA Annual Publication; Indian Herbal Pharmacopoeia; IDMA-APA Forum, for professional pharmaceutical analysts; IDMA-PEG Newsletter, for pharmaceutical engineers; and Technical Monographs, guidelines on standards in manufacture. IDMA has also instituted several awards for excellence in various fields of pharmaceuticals, including patents and research, and for outstanding and young analysts.

Source: IDMA Website, https://idma-assn.org.

Note 8: Extension of Patent Term

Japan's Patent Act, Article 67

1. The duration of a patent right shall expire after a period of 20 years from the filing date of the patent application.
2. Where there is a period during which the patented invention is unable to be worked because approvals prescribed by relevant Acts that are intended to ensure the safely, etc. or any other disposition designated by Cabinet Order as requiring considerable time for the proper execution of the disposition in light of the purpose, procedures, etc., of such a disposition is necessary to obtain for the working of the patented invention, the duration of the patent right may be extended, upon the filing of a request for registration of extension of the duration, by a period not exceeding 5 years.

Source: http://www.japaneselawtranslation.go.jp/law/detail/?printID=&ft=1&co=01&x=32&y=19&ky=%E7%89%B9%E8%A8%B1%E6%B3%95&page=10&id=42&lvm=&re=02&vm=02.

Note 9: Mailbox

For **pharmaceutical** and **agricultural chemical** products, the country must accept the *filing* of patent applications from the beginning of the transitional period (1995), even though the decision on whether or not to grant any patent itself need not be taken until the end of the transitional period (TRIPS Article 70.8). This scheme is called the "mailbox" provision.

Source: WTO Website, "Do members have any obligations under the agreement during the transition period?"

https://www.wto.org/english/tratop_e/trips_e/tripfq_e.htm#Transition.

Note 10: EMR

If the government allows the relevant pharmaceutical or agricultural chemical product to be marketed during the transition period, it must—subject to certain conditions—provide the patent applicant an exclusive marketing right for the product for 5 years or until a decision on granting a product patent is taken, whichever is shorter (TRIPS Article 70.9).

Source: WTO Website, "Do members have any obligations under the agreement during the transition period? https://www.wto.org/english/tratop_e/trips_e/tripfq_e.htm#Transition.

Note 11: Term of Protection

TRIPS Article 33

"Term of Protection": The term of protection available shall not end before the expiration of a period of 20 years counted from the filing date.

Source: WTO Website, https://www.wto.org/english/docs_e/legal_e/27-trips_04c_e.htm.

Terminology

#1 Product Patent

A product patent is an exclusive right given to the original inventor of a product. This means that no other manufacturer can provide the same product through the same or any other process. The implication is that the producer will not have a competitor as it is the product which is patented. The product patent system gives a higher level of protection to the inventor as there will not be any other patent holder. TRIPS follows the product patent regime.

Source: IndianEconomy.Net Website, http://www.indianeconomy.net/splclassroom/98/what-is-the-differencebetween-product-patent-and-process.

#2 Generic Drug

A generic drug is the same as a brand-name drug in terms of dosage, safety, strength, how it is taken, quality, performance, and intended use. Before approving a generic pharmaceutical product, the FDA requires many rigorous tests and procedures to assure that the generic drug can be substituted for the brand-name drug. The FDA bases evaluations of substitutability, or "therapeutic equivalence," of generic drugs on scientific evaluations. By law, a generic pharmaceutical product must contain the identical amounts of the same active ingredient(s) as the brand-name product. Pharmaceutical products evaluated as "therapeutically equivalent" can be expected to have equal effect and no difference when substituted for the brand-name product.

Source: "Drugs@FDA Glossary of Terms," http://www.fda.gov/Drugs/InformationOnDrugs/ucm079436.htm.

#3 Reverse Engineering

The act of copying the product of another company by looking carefully at how it is made.

Source: *Cambridge Dictionary*, http://dictionary.cambridge.org/dictionary/english/reverse-engineering.

Y. Mitsumori, *The Indian Pharmaceutical Industry*,
SpringerBriefs in Health Care Management and Economics,
https://doi.org/10.1007/978-981-10-6790-7

#4 Branded Generic Drugs
Generic drugs for which a pharmaceutical manufacturing company has attached its brand name and may have invested in its marketing to differentiate it from other generic brands.

Source: Pharmaceuticals Export Promotion Council of India (Pharmexcil) Website, http://pharmexcil.org/uploadfile/ufiles/1535226443_definitions.pdf.

#5 Brand-Name Drug
A brand-name drug is a drug marketed under a proprietary, trademark-protected name. Innovator drugs are patented by MNC pharmaceutical companies to prevent their being copied or reverse-engineered by other companies.

Source: Pharmaceuticals Export Promotion Council of India (Pharmexcil) Website, http://pharmexcil.org/uploadfile/ufiles/1535226443_definitions.pdf.

#6 Médecins Sans Frontières (MSF)/Doctors Without Borders
Médecins Sans Frontières (MSF)/Doctors Without Borders is a private, international association. The association is made up mainly of doctors and health sector workers and is also open to all other professions which might help in achieving its aims. All of its members agree to honor the following principles: MSF provides assistance to populations in distress, to victims of natural or man-made disasters, and to victims of armed conflict. It does so irrespective of race, religion, creed, or political convictions. MSF observes neutrality and impartiality in the name of universal medical ethics and the right to humanitarian assistance and claims full and unhindered freedom in the exercise of its functions. Members undertake to respect their professional code of ethics and maintain complete independence from all political, economic, or religious powers.

Source: Médecins Sans Frontières Website, https:www.doctorswithoutborders.org.

#7 Patented Drug
A patented drug is a drug to which a patent pertains. A patent provides exclusive rights to the patent holder to use the invention for the duration of the patent.

Source: Patented Medicine Prices Review Board, Government of Canada (partially modified),

http://www.pmprb-cepmb.gc.ca/about-us/frequently-asked-questions.

#8 Drug Development Pipeline
A drug development pipeline is the set of compounds, for instance, drugs in development, that a pharmaceutical company has under development at any given point in time.

Source: Weblio Website, http://ejje.weblio.jp/content/Drug+pipeline.

#9 High Impact Factor
The impact factor, proposed by Eugene Garfield, is the ratio between citations and recent citable items published. Thus, the impact factor of a journal is calculated by dividing the number of current year citations to the source items published in that journal during the previous 2 years by the number of published articles in that

journal during the previous 2 years. *Journal Citation Reports* calculates and publishes the annual impact factors for journals. A higher impact factor generally indicates that this journal's articles have been cited more.

Source: NIH Website, http://nihlibrary.campusguides.com/c.php?g=38330&p=244518.

#10 US Food and Drug Administration (FDA)
The Food and Drug Administration (FDA) is an agency within the US Department of Health and Human Services. It consists of the Office of the Commissioner and four directorates overseeing the core functions of the agency: Medical Products and Tobacco, Foods and Veterinary Medicine, Global Regulatory Operations and Policy, and Operations. The FDA is responsible for protecting the public health by assuring the safety, effectiveness, quality, and security of human and veterinary drugs, vaccines and other biological products, and medical devices.

Source: FDA Website, https://www.fda.gov/AboutFDA/Transparency/Basics/ucm192695.htm.

#11 Abbreviated New Drug Application (ANDA)
An Abbreviated New Drug Application (ANDA) contains data that, when submitted to the FDA's Center for Drug Evaluation and Research, Office of Generic Drugs, provides for the review and ultimate approval of a generic drug product. Generic drug applications are called "abbreviated" because they are generally not required to include preclinical (animal) and clinical (human) data to establish safety and effectiveness. Instead, a generic applicant must scientifically demonstrate that its product is bioequivalent (i.e., performs in the same manner as the innovator drug). Once approved, an applicant may manufacture and market the generic drug product to provide a safe, effective, low-cost alternative to the American public.

Source: "Drugs@FDA Glossary of Terms," http://www.fda.gov/Drugs/InformationOnDrugs/ucm079436.htm.

#12 Drug Master File (DMF)
A drug master file (DMF) is a confidential, detailed document submitted by Active Pharmaceutical Ingredient (API) manufacturers to the FDA. A DMF contains the chemistry, manufacturing, and controls of a drug component. A DMF is required to supply bulk materials to the US, but the FDA does not require all manufacturers to submit a DMF. However, the information contained in a DMF may be used to support an Investigational New Drug Application (IND), a New Drug Application (NDA), an ANDA, another DMF, an Export Application, or related documents.

Source: The Balance, "What Is a Drug Master File (DMF)?" https://www.thebalance.com/drug-master-file-dmf-2663082.

#13 Clinical Trial
A research study in which one or more human subjects are prospectively assigned to one or more interventions (which may include placebo or other control) to evaluate the effects of those interventions on health-related biomedical or behavioral outcomes.

Phase I. Test a new biomedical intervention in a small group of people (e.g., 20–80) for the first time to determine efficacy and evaluate safety (e.g., determine a safe dosage range and identify side effects).

Phase II. Study the biomedical or behavioral intervention in a larger group of people (several hundred) to determine efficacy and further evaluate safety.

Phase III. Study to determine efficacy of the biomedical or behavioral intervention in large groups of people (from several hundred to several thousand) by comparing the intervention to other standard or experimental interventions, as well as to monitor adverse effects and to collect information that will allow the interventions to be used safely.

Phase IV. Studies conducted after the intervention has been marketed. These studies are designed to monitor the effectiveness of the approved intervention in the general population and to collect information about any adverse effects associated with widespread use.

Source: "NIH Glossary & Acronym List," https://grants.nih.gov/grants/glossary.htm#C.

#14 New Drug Application (NDA)

When the sponsor of a new drug believes that enough evidence of the drug's safety and effectiveness has been obtained to meet the FDA's requirements for marketing approval, the sponsor submits to the FDA a new drug application (NDA). The application must contain data from specific technical viewpoints for review, including chemistry, pharmacology, medical, biopharmaceutics, and statistics. If the NDA is approved, the product may be marketed in the USA. For internal tracking purposes, all NDAs are assigned an NDA number.

Source: "Drugs@FDA Glossary of Terms," http://www.fda.gov/Drugs/InformationOnDrugs/ucm079436.htm.

#15 Cross-licensing

Gives one party a license to use (patented or copyright material) in return for a similar license.

Source: Oxford Dictionaries Website, https://en.oxforddictionaries.com/definition/us/cross-license.

#16 Acute Disease

A disease which is characterized by a single or repeated episode of relatively rapid onset and short duration from which the patient usually returns to his or her normal or previous state or level of activity. An acute episode of a chronic disease—for example, an episode of diabetic coma in a patient with diabetes—is often treated as an acute disease.

Source: WHO, "A Glossary of Terms for Community Health Care and Services for Older Persons" (report, WHO Centre for Health Development, Ageing and Health Technical Report, vol. 5, 2004), http://apps.who.int/iris/bitstream/10665/68896/1/WHO_WKC_Tech.Ser._04.2.pdf.

#17 Chronic Disease

A disease which has one or more of the following characteristics: is permanent, leaves residual disability, is caused by nonreversible pathological alternation, requires special training of the patient for rehabilitation, or may be expected to require a long period of supervision, observation, or care.

Source: WHO, "A Glossary of Terms for Community Health Care and Services for Older Persons" (report, WHO Centre for Health Development, Ageing and Health Technical, vol. 5, 2004), http://apps.who.int/iris/bitstream/10665/68896/1/WHO_WKC_Tech.Ser._04.2.pdf.

#18 Welfare Loss

Welfare loss is the loss of total societal welfare (consumer and produce surplus) that occurs when a market is producing at a level of output that is not socially optimal (where MSB=MSC). It may arise from a market failure or from a government intervention in an already efficient market.

Source: Welker's Wikinomics, "Economics in Plain English: For Students and Teachers of Economics," http://welkerswikinomics.com/blog/glossary/deadweight-loss.

#19 Blockbuster

Pharmaceutical Industry jargon for a product with very large sales—usually US$1 billion or higher—and on the back of which new product development can be funded. Examples: the antiulcer drug Zantac was a major blockbuster for Glaxo and the antidepressant Prozac was a major blockbuster for Eli Lilly.

Source: Cheri Grace, "The Effect of Changing Intellectual Property on Pharmaceutical Industry Prospects in India and China: Considerations for Access to Medicines," *DFID Health Systems Resource Centre* (June 2004)

#20 Drug Delivery Systems (DDS)

Drug delivery systems are engineered technologies for the targeted delivery and/or controlled release of therapeutic agents.

Source: National Institute of Biomedical Imaging and Bioengineering (NIBIB), https://www.nibib.nih.gov/science-education/science-topics/drug-delivery-systems-getting-drugs-their-targets-controlled-manner.

#21 Good Manufacturing Practice (GMP)

A GMP is a system for ensuring that products are consistently produced and controlled according to quality standards. It is designed to minimize the risks involved in any pharmaceutical production that cannot be eliminated through testing the final product. GMP covers all aspects of production from the starting materials, premises, and equipment to the training and personal hygiene of staff. Detailed, written procedures are essential for each process that could affect the quality of the finished product. There must be systems to provide documented proof that correct procedures are consistently followed at each step in the manufacturing process—every time a product is made.

Source: The International Society for Pharmaceutical Engineering (ISPE) Website, http://www.ispe.org/gmp-resources.

#22 Quinolones

Quinolones are synthetic, bactericidal antibiotics that are broad spectrum. They inhibit the enzyme topoisomerase II, a DNA gyrase that is necessary for the replication of bacteria. The FDA has advised that quinolones should only be used to treat conditions such as sinusitis, bronchitis, and uncomplicated urinary tract infections when other, less toxic antibiotics are not appropriate. Quinolones have been associated with severe and potentially permanent side effects that may involve the tendons, muscles, joints, nerves, and central nervous system. Quinolones are not recommended to be used in children and adolescents under the age of 18 years.

Source: Drugs.com, https://www.drugs.com/drug-class/quinolones.html.

#23 Evergreening

Evergreening is a term that describes techniques employed by pharmaceutical companies to take advantage of loopholes in the patent and regulatory systems in order to artificially extend the market monopoly of a product beyond its legitimate period. It is the strategy applied by the innovator company to obtain the multiple patents that cover the different aspects of the same product.

Source: Pharmainfo.net, http://www.pharmainfo.net/manandkumar/evergreening-patents-emerging-issue.

#24 Process Patent

The process patent is granted for a particular manufacturing process, and not for the product itself. Any other person can produce the same product through some other process, modifying the various parameters. The implication is that there will be more than one producer for the same product because of the possibility of different processes for manufacturing of the product. A weakness of the process patent regime is that it gives less protection for the inventor. There is a high tendency for competitors to re-engineer the original invention by discovering a new process with less work and investment. A benefit of the process patent regime is that it reduces the element of monopoly.

Source: Indianeconomy.com Website, http://www.indianeconomy.net/splclassroom/98/what-is-the-differencebetween-product-patent-and-process.

#25 International Patent Classification (IPC)

The International Patent Classification, which is commonly referred to as "the IPC," is based on an international multilateral treaty administered by WIPO. It is an internationally recognized patent classification system, which provides a common classification for patents according to technology groups. The IPC is a hierarchical system in which the whole area of technology is divided into a range of sections, classes, subclasses, and groups. There are eight sections which are broken down into classes and subclasses. The IPC is periodically revised in order to improve the system and to take account of technical development. The current (eighth) edition of the IPC came into force on January 1, 2006.

Source: OECD, "Glossary of Patent Terminology" (Economic Analysis and Statistics Division, Directorate for Science, Technology and Industry), https://www.oecd.org/sti/sci-tech/37569498.pdf.

The manufacturer's authorised representative in the EU is Springer Nature Customer Service Centre GmbH, Europaplatz 3, 69115 Heidelberg, Germany. If you have any concerns regarding our products, please contact ProductSafety@springernature.com

Printed and bound by CPI Group (UK) Ltd, Croydon, CR0 4YY
01/10/2026
02225882-0006